W9-BLG-779

HUMANIST
ANTHOLOGY

HUMANIST ANTHOLOGY

FROM CONFUCIUS TO ATTENBOROUGH

EDITED BY **MARGARET KNIGHT**

REVISED BY **JAMES HERRICK**

PREFACE BY EDWARD BLISHEN

 **Prometheus Books**

59 John Glenn Drive
Amherst, NewYork 14228-2197

11-8-2007
LAN
Gift

Published 1995 by Prometheus Books
in association with the Rationalist Press Association

99 98 97 96 95   5 4 3 2 1

Library of Congress Cataloging-in-Publication Data

Humanist anthology / edited by Margaret Knight. — Rev. / by James Herrick.
   p. cm.
   Includes bibliographical references.
   ISBN 0-87975-957-7 (hbk.)
   1. Humanism. 2. Ethics. 3. Religion. I. Knight, Margaret, 1903–1983.
II. Herrick, James.
B821.H6915   1995
144—dc20   95-42599
                                                 CIP

Printed in the United States of America on acid-free paper.

O genus infelix humanum, talia divis
cum tribuit facta atque iras adjunxit acerbas!
quantos tum gemitus ipsi sibi, quantaque nobis
volnera, quas lacrimas peperere minoribu' nostris!
nec pietas ullast velatum saepe videri
vertier ad lapidem atque omnis accedere ad aras
nec procumbere humi prostratum et pandere palmas
ante deum delubra nec aras sanguine multo
spargere quadrupedum nec votis nectere vota,
sed mage pacata posse omnia mente tueri.

Lucretius, *De Rerum Natura,* vv. 1194–1203

> Oh, unhappy human kind,
> In those grim gods, your own creation,
> What anguish for yourselves you find,
> For babes unborn what tribulation!
> Not palms in prostrate prayer outspread,
> Not all the blood on altars shed
> Is piety, but that calm mind,
> Whose fruit is tranquil contemplation.

Translation by J. S. L. Gilmour and R. E. Latham

CONTENTS

PREFACE

A huge number of years ago, aged fourteen, I was conducting a correspondence with a gentle ass, as I now think of him, who was attempting to prevent my secession from a very odd religious group called the Crusaders. This group existed for those who might in a tangled way be described as public and private school-boys: but it didn't frown on recruits from the grammar schools. I had landed briefly with them in my flight from a Methodist Sunday School: and my growing perception that the readiness to be irra-tional that seemed to be at the heart of religious attitudes was not for me, was strengthened by the behaviour of the Crusaders. They were encouraged largely to shout, with enormous loud-ness, what could only be described as religious rugby football songs, mixed with other chants that drew upon (as I saw it) infa-mous military imagery. I thought, with the panic of an adolescent who found himself isolated in his thinking, that it all represented a retreat from the true gravity of things: I was appalled already by what I knew of the association of religion with torment and mas-sacre, and by its invention in this form or that of the idea that those who failed to adhere to a particular belief were damned and doomed: in the view of my gentle ass, indeed, condemned to everlasting agony. So I wrote to him my floundering letters of dis-may: and in one reply he said you could appreciate the beauty of the stained glass in a cathedral only if you came and stood inside it. I said in answer to that that he might as well be saying one could understand the misery of being a prisoner only by having oneself locked up in a jail. I drew as much as I could on the little I'd then read of the literature that made my thoughts and feelings articulate: but I didn't know how much of that there was: and there was no *Humanist Anthology* for me to stumble upon.

Margaret Knight set out to assemble this anthology in the light of the idea (among other ideas) that it would counter the illu-sion that love and human brotherhood were purely Christian con-ceptions, and were unknown in the pagan world. As I made my way through the anthology in its renewed form, the beleaguered fourteen-year-old I was seized upon the evidence that makes this case with the eagerness it would have caused him had he been able to read the collection sixty years ago. It is the great calm spread of an uninterruptedly benign rationality across millennia that is so striking when these voices are gathered in this fashion. That, together with the obvious conclusion one has to draw, that here is a procession of assertions that come from often markedly different quarters of the mind (or the heart), without there being the least suggestion that such differences might be occasions for war, terrorism, detention, torture or excommunication.

The revisions here, the droppings and the addings, make, I think, for an increased lightness: not in the sense of the effect being less considerable, but in its being somehow swifter, brighter. Voices from the past thirty years are admitted, of course: but it's not simply that, for me: it is that the dancing, witty nature of humanism seems more to the fore. Humanists can be as solid in argument as anybody, and not all argument is capable of being made sprightly. But how often, here, ringing words are found for humane perceptions. There's D'Holbach's 'How can we receive for our model a being, whose divine virtues are precisely the opposite of human virtues?' There's George Eliot's verdict on the morally and intellectually lazy: that the one thing they are staunch for 'is the utmost liberty of private haziness' (If only I'd had that phrase to level at my gentle ass, whose fervour I at last discovered was a mask for his horror of deep inquiry). There's Mark Twain looking with a sort of stern comedy at the idea that the inventor of a benign system might invent the fly as part of it. There's Diderot's marvellous pocket allegory about the man who, seeking revenge for the cruelty of his neighbours, invented the idea of God. There is W. K. Clifford making a memorable statement of one of the essential attitudes of the humanist—perhaps the most essential: 'If I let myself believe something on insufficient evidence, there may be no great harm done by the mere belief. . . . But I cannot help doing this great wrong towards Man, that I make myself credulous. . . . The danger to society is not merely that it should believe wrong things . . . but that it should become credulous, and lose the habit of testing things and inquiring into them; for then it must sink back into savagery.' And there is Montaigne, at a time of great religious insanity making his sane assertion: 'It is putting a very high value on one's conjectures to roast a man alive on the strength of them.' But then, as for E. M. Forster (who spoke of his preferred temple as standing in 'that Elysian field where even the immoral are admitted'), my law-givers are Erasmus and Montaigne, not Moses and St. Paul.

I have to add, as a man in his mid-seventies, that if the anthology offers a long tradition of facing life with all possible courage and honesty of mind, it offers such a tradition, too, in the matter of facing death. I am cheered in my perishing bones by David Hume, who said he could not well imagine what excuses he could make to Charon in order to obtain a little delay. And I am grateful for a perception I had at fourteen, that is now most serviceable in removing all possibility of obscene panic rooted in the religious view of things, and that was most trenchantly expressed by Charles Darwin, quoted here: 'I can indeed hardly see how anyone ought to wish Christianity to be true: for if so the plain language of the text seems to show that the men who do not believe, and this would include my Father, Brother and almost all my best friends, will be everlastingly punished.'

At fourteen, I would have given anything to have the *Humanist Anthology*; at 74, I am deeply glad to have it.

EDWARD BLISHEN

Hadley Wood, 1995

INTRODUCTION

'The meaning of a word,' said Wittgenstein, 'is the way in which it is used': and the meaning, thus defined, of the word 'humanist' has changed appreciably since the turn of the century. Today, to describe someone as a humanist does not usually imply that he has been educated in *litterae humaniores*. Rather, it implies that he sees no reason for believing in a supernatural God, or in a life after death; that he holds that man must face his problems with his own intellectual and moral resources, without invoking supernatural aid; and that authority, supernatural or otherwise, should not be allowed to obstruct inquiry in any field of thought.

With these basic beliefs there go commonly two corollaries. First, that virtue is a matter of promoting human well-being, not of obeying the commands of a supposed superhuman lawgiver; and, second, that the mainsprings of moral action are what Darwin called the social instincts—those altruistic, co-operative tendencies that are as much part of our innate biological equipment as are our tendencies towards aggression and cruelty.

Though the terminology has altered, there is of course nothing new in these doctrines. Humanism derives from a far older tradition than Christianity. The great classical civilizations of China, Greece and Rome were rooted in humanist values; and though these values were obscured in Europe during the long night of the Dark Ages they shone forth with renewed brilliance at the Renaissance, and have gathered fresh strength today in alliance with the mighty power of Science.

The impulse to compile this anthology arose primarily from my recent contacts with students. In 1955 I gave two broadcasts on 'Morals without Religion' which (in the words of *Time* magazine) nearly lifted the roof off Broadcasting House; and since then I have frequently lectured, spoken in debates and talked informally about humanism to undergraduates in most of the British universities.

The experience has been enlightening as well as stimulating. I found that few even of the most humanistically minded students

19

had read Hume, Mill, Huxley or the other classical sceptics, though they were often keenly interested when they heard them quoted; while the Christians (still a majority, though a diminishing one) had not only not read these writers, but were serenely convinced that, whatever their arguments were, they had all been refuted—though they were vague as to how or by whom. Many knew little or nothing about the historical background of Humanism (or, indeed, Christianity) and wished to know more. So I felt increasingly that it would be a good thing if the humanist classics, of the pre-Christian as well as the Christian eras, could be made more accessible to the general reader.

The present book is a contribution to this end. The passages it contains are all humanist in their general outlook, though they do not, of course, represent an established body of doctrine which all humanists accept. The book will, I hope, indicate how rich is the tradition from which present-day humanism derives. It may also remove some misconceptions—in particular, the illusion (much encouraged by the Religious Broadcasting Department of the BBC) that love and human brotherhood are purely Christian conceptions and were unknown in the pagan world.

In selecting extracts for inclusion I encountered (as would be expected) borderline cases where it was difficult to decide whether a writer could fairly be classed as a humanist. The open rejection of the prevailing religion has in most periods of history been a somewhat risky procedure, and sceptical writers have often judged it prudent to write their scepticism between the lines, or to make ironic or purely formal protestations of orthodoxy. I have not excluded any writer merely because he took these precautions; and I have included, also, some writers who spoke respectfully of 'God' and 'religion' but who used the terms in unusual senses (such as Spinoza, who equated God with the universe, and Einstein, who said 'I believe in Spinoza's God' and who used 'religion' as a synonym for the disinterested pursuit of truth).

The most difficult problems arose with Voltaire and Thomas Paine. They were genuine Deists, and so do not, strictly speaking, qualify for inclusion: yet historically they contributed so much to the growth of humanism that it seemed unthinkable to leave them out. I decided eventually to include them, though with some qualms.

Among pre-Christian writers, I had no hesitation in including the Epicureans, who held that gods exist but that they are quite unconcerned about human well-being or morals. The Stoics are nearer the borderline; but their ethical code was essentially Humanist, and their cosmology (a somewhat nebulous pantheism, in which all human minds were regarded as forming part of the Logos, variously defined as Reason or Creative Force) is not incompatible with humanism, though no humanist would accept it today. Incidentally, Canon Charles Raven, in a recent broadcast, referred to Gallio,* the brother of Seneca, as 'the gentle Gallio—the Stoic, or, as we should now say, the scientific humanist', so I can claim Christian support for my classification.

The selections dated A.D. include a good deal of anti-Christian polemic. For this I make no apology. When a writer is urging that the traditional system of ethics and cosmology should be replaced by another, he must do more than simply expound the system he advocates; he must also explain why he thinks the current system needs changing. This certainly appears to have been the view of the founder of Christianity, who devoted a large part of his teaching to denouncing the errors of the Scribes and Pharisees. And denouncing them, incidentally, in far from temperate language. 'Woe unto you, Scribes and Pharisees, hypocrites! for ye are like unto whited sepulchres, which indeed appear beautiful outward, but within are full of dead men's bones, and of all uncleanness. . . . Ye serpents, ye generation of vipers, how can ye escape the damnation of Hell?'† None of the humanist writers I have quoted has applied quite such forceful terms to his Christian opponents.

My thanks are due to Dr. John Gilmour and Mr. R. E. Latham for permission to quote their verse translation of the passage from Lucretius that I have used as an epigraph; to Dr. Gilmour again for introducing me to the writings of Jean Meslier, and lending me a very rare copy of Voltaire's *Extrait du Testament de Jean Meslier*; to Dr. Victor Purcell for directing my reading of the Chinese classics; to my husband for his unfailing interest and encouragement; to Aberdeen University Library, without whose

---

*The Listener, September 5, 1957.
†Cf. Acts, xviii, 12–17.

facilities the work of compilation would have been greatly increased; and to the many publishers and others (listed fully on pp. 219–220), who have given permission for the reproduction of copyright material.

MARGARET KNIGHT

Aberdeen, 1961

NOTE.—When there are a number of extracts from a single author they are usually in chronological order, or (if from the same book) in the order in which they appear; but I have not kept strictly to this principle when considerations of subject or sequence favoured a different arrangement.

The dates given for books are those of the first edition; in the case of translations, of the first edition in the original language.

Footnotes from the original texts are numbered. Editorial footnotes are indicated by an asterisk and followed by (Ed). The subject-headings to the extracts do not form part of the original texts.

FOREWORD

This anthology, first published in 1961, has sold steadily since that year, until it recently went out of print. We decided to take the opportunity of reprinting to revise the anthology and bring in a new preface. About 30 per cent of the material is new, so it is well worth obtaining by those who have the original anthology, but it remains in content and outlook essentially Margaret Knight's anthology.

Margaret Knight was a remarkable humanist who did much in the 1950s and 1960s to present humanism to the public at a time when there was a burgeoning interest in the humanist outlook. She laid a strong emphasis on the tradition of morality without God. In this anthology that has been kept, but we have added more comments on science and a few slightly more literary entries (Heinrich Heine, George Eliot's *Adam Bede*, Mark Twain). A few entries come from a more European philosophical tradition, such as Nietzsche and Sartre. We have gone outside the European tradition to include Averroës, not a full humanist, but a rare Islamic sceptic. India has a strong atheistic tradition going back to ancient Hindu texts and I have included two important twentieth-century Indian humanists—M. N. Roy and Gora.

This humanist anthology is important and valuable for (at least) two reasons. First, the debate about the gods, the human position in the universe, the purpose of life, and so on, is not complete. Many of these extracts provide insight into that continuous debate. Second, the humanist anthology substantiates the humanist tradition. A movement aware of its past carries more weight and power than one without. The movement that loses its tradition loses its memory and substance. Much of the humanist tradition is invisible and resides in folk tales and carvings or in writings which deliberately obscure their full implication for the sake of the safety of the writer. It is therefore all the more important to value that fine written tradition which we have.

The anthology is arranged chronologically except for the last two items by Jacob Bronowski and David Attenborough, which

23

provide a fitting conclusion. Bronowski takes on Auschwitz—a fact about human behaviour which humanists in the twentieth century cannot ignore and which may make us less optimistic than humanists of earlier periods. Attenborough points out that we have no special place in the universe, yet we have 'an awesome responsibility': 'In our hands now lies not only our own future, but that of all other living creatures with whom we share the earth.' May the humanist tradition here represented help us to come to terms with the nature of humanity and give us the strength and insight to take on the 'awesome responsibility' of our planet's future.

I am grateful for assistance from Antony Chapman, David Pollock and Nicolas Walter during the preparation of this revised anthology.

JAMES HERRICK

Wanborough, 1995

CONFUCIUS (K'ung Fu-tzu)*
551–479 B.C.

Good Behaviour

The Master said, A young man's duty is to behave well to his parents at home and to his elders abroad, to be cautious in giving promises and punctual in keeping them, to have kindly feelings towards everyone, but seek the intimacy of the Good. If, when all this is done, he has any energy to spare, then let him study the polite arts.

Analects, I, 6, trans. Arthur Waley

The Master said, (the good man) does not grieve that other people do not recognize his merits. His only anxiety is lest he should fail to recognize theirs.

Ibid., I, 16

The Master said, A gentleman takes as much trouble to discover what is right as lesser men take to discover what will pay.

Ibid., IV,16

Jan Jung asked about goodness. The Master said, Behave when away from home as though you were in the presence of an important guest. Deal with the common people as though you were officiating at an important sacrifice. Do not do to others what you would not like yourself. Then there will be no feelings of opposition to you, whether it is the affairs of a State that you are handling or the affairs of a family.

Ibid., XII

Someone said, What do you say concerning the principle that injury should be recompensed with kindness? The Master said,

*The Analects is a collection of sayings in the Confucian tradition. They are traditionally ascribed to Confucius himself, but probably few of them contain his actual words. (Ed.)

With what then will you recompense kindness? Recompense injury with justice, and recompense kindness with kindness.

Ibid., XIV, 36, trans. James Legge

The Art of Government

Tzu-Chang asked, What must a man do, that he may thereby be fitted to govern the land? The Master said, He must pay attention to the Five Lovely Things and put away from him the Four Ugly Things. Tzu-Chang said, What are they, that you call the Five Lovely Things? The Master said, A gentleman can be bounteous without extravagance, can get work out of people without arousing resentment, has longings but is never covetous, is proud but never insolent, inspires awe but is never ferocious. . . .

Tzu-Chang said, What are they, that you call the Four Ugly Things? The Master said, Putting men to death without having taught them (the right); that is called savagery. Expecting the completion of tasks, without giving due warning; that is called oppression. To be dilatory about giving orders, but to expect absolute punctuality; that is called being a tormentor. And similarly, though meaning to let a man have something, to be grudging about bringing it out from within; that is called behaving like a petty functionary.

Ibid., XX, 2, trans. Arthur Waley

THUCYDIDES
c. 471–401 B.C.

Funeral Oration of Pericles

Extracts from the speech made by Pericles, Chief Minister of Athens, at the funeral of the Athenians who fell in the first year of the Peloponnesian War, 431 B.C.

Our government is not copied from those of other states: we are a model to them, rather than they to us. Our constitution is called a democracy, because power is in the hands, not of the few, but of the many. The law treats all men alike in their private disputes:

and when public honours and public offices are awarded, it is on grounds of merit alone, not because a man belongs to a particular class or party. If a man has the capacity to serve the state, he is never kept in obscurity because he is poor.

In our personal relationships, we have the same free and tolerant spirit. We are not suspicious of one another, not indignant with our neighbours if they enjoy life in their own way; we do not give them sour looks which annoy people, even though they do them no injury. We are free in our private lives, but in public affairs we are law-abiding. We respect those whom we put in positions of authority, and we obey the laws, particularly those which protect man from oppression: and we respect, too, those unwritten laws which are not in the statute book, but which we count it shameful to break.

And furthermore: we have not forgotten to provide recreation for mind and spirit when work is done. We have regular games and sacrifices the whole year through, and our homes have a taste and beauty which delight the eye and drive away care. Because of the greatness of our city, the fruits of the whole earth flow into it, so that we enjoy the produce of other countries as freely as our own.

Then in military matters we are more liberal than our adversaries. Our city is thrown open to the world; we never have wholesale deportations of aliens, or prevent them from seeing or hearing anything which it would be to an enemy's advantage to know. We rely, not on secret preparations or stratagems, but on our own active energy. And it is the same in our education. While they (the Spartans) are subjected from childhood to a laborious training in order to make them brave, we Athenians live at ease; but that does not stop us from going out to meet the same dangers as the Spartans face. . . .

There is much to be said, I think, for our way of meeting danger lightheartedly, with natural courage rather than with courage that has been drilled into us. It has the advantage that we do not meet trouble half-way: yet when hardship and suffering come, we face them just as bravely as those who are for ever preparing for them.

And there are other respects, too, in which our city deserves admiration. We are lovers of beauty, yet our tastes are simple; we delight in intellectual pursuits, yet we are not soft. Wealth we employ for use, not for ostentation or boasting. We think it no shame for a man to be poor; the only shame is in not taking active steps to escape from poverty. Our public men do not neglect their domestic concerns: and private citizens, even those who are mainly occupied with their own affairs, are still reasonably good judges of public policy. For we are not like some other nations. If a man takes no interest in politics, we do not praise him for minding his own business—we say he is a bad citizen. We, ordinary Athenians, either criticize public affairs, or at least have a sound grasp of them.

We do not regard discussion as a hindrance to action: the greatest hindrance is to rush into action without adequate knowledge. In this respect, too, we are unlike other nations; for when we take risks, we take them with open eyes, whereas others are brave through ignorance, and grow afraid when they stop to think. And the bravest man, surely, is he who can see quite clearly what is painful, what pleasant, in life, yet who does not on that account shrink from danger. . . .

Such, then, is the city for which these men, resolved that she should not be taken from them, nobly fought and nobly died. . . . Surely a death such as theirs gives the true measure of a man's worth. . . . Even those who had many faults can justly plead the valour with which they fought for their country: they have blotted out evil with good, and done more service to the state at the last than they ever did harm before. Not one of these men shrank back: not the rich because he wanted to go on enjoying his wealth, not the poor because he longed for a future day when his fortunes would change. . . . They put aside their personal hopes. . . . They limited their view to the task which lay before their eyes, and thought it better to die in defeating their foes, than to surrender and save their lives. So they fled only from dishonour, and with their bodies stood out the battle; and thus, triumphant over fear, in a moment, at the crisis of their fate, they were swept away.

Such were these men: they were true Athenians. You who are left may hope to escape their fate, but must resolve to show a no less bold spirit against the enemy. Such a spirit is useful in battle, but I need not dwell on this, for you know it as well as I do. And it is not just a matter of knowledge, or of weighing advantages. I would have you day by day fix your eyes on the greatness of Athens, until the love of her fills your hearts: and when you realize her greatness, reflect that it was built by men such as these: men who knew their duty, and were governed in their actions by a sense of honour: men who, if they failed in an enterprise, resolved that at least Athens should not find them failing in courage, and gave freely the best offering that they could. They gave her their lives, to her and to all of us: and in return they won, for themselves, fame that grows not old, and the most splendid of sepulchres—not the sepulchre in which their bodies are laid, but where their glory survives for ever in men's minds. . . .

I shall not, therefore, commiserate with those parents of the dead who stand here. I shall rather try to console them. You know the uncertainty of life: and you know that those who have won honour must be deemed fortunate—even though it be an honourable death, like your sons', or an honourable grief, like your own. That the end of happiness and the end of life should come together—this is good fortune. I know that this is a hard saying. The sight of others' happiness will often remind you of what you once enjoyed. . . . But those of you who are still of an age to become parents must be patient in the hope of having more children, who will prevent you from brooding on those that have gone. To Athens these children will be doubly precious—both as filling the empty places, and as a source of security too: for men take more responsible views on public affairs when they have children whose safety is at stake. And to those of you who are now too old to have children, I would say: rejoice that you have been happy for most of your lives, and reflect that what remains is not long: and let the fair fame of the dead be your consolation.

History of the Peloponnesian War, Book II, 37–44
Translation by Benjamin Jowett, adapted by M. K.

EPICURUS
342–270 B.C.

Death

Become accustomed to the belief that death is nothing to us. For all good and evil consists in sensation, but death is deprivation of sensation. And therefore a right understanding that death is nothing to us makes the mortality of life enjoyable, not because it adds to it an infinite span of time, but because it takes away the craving for immortality. For there is nothing terrible in life for the man who has truly comprehended that there is nothing terrible in not living.

Letter to Menoeceus, 124–5, trans. Cyril Bailey

Against all else it is possible to provide security, but as against death all of us mortals alike dwell in an unfortified city.

Fragments, 31

Pleasure

We call pleasure the beginning and end of the blessed life. For we recognize pleasure as the first good innate in us, and from pleasure we begin every act of choice and avoidance, and to pleasure we return again, using the feeling as the standard by which we judge every good. . . .

When therefore we maintain that pleasure is the end, we do not mean the pleasures of profligates and those that consist in sensuality, as is supposed by some who are either ignorant or disagree with us or do not understand, but freedom from pain in the body and from trouble in the mind. For it is not continuous drinkings and revellings, nor the satisfaction of lusts, nor the enjoyment of fish and other luxuries of the wealthy table, which produce a pleasant life, but sober reasoning, searching out the motives for all choice and avoidance, and banishing mere opinions, to which are due the greatest disturbance of the spirit.

Letter to Menoeceus, 128–9, 131–2

Superstition

A man cannot dispel his fear about the most important matters if he does not know what is the nature of the universe but suspects the truth of some mythical story. So that without natural science it is not possible to attain our pleasures unalloyed.

Principal Doctrines, 12

Friendship

Of all the things which wisdom acquires to produce the blessedness of the complete life, far the greatest is the possession of
friendship.

ibid., 27

It is not so much our friends' help that supports us, as the confidence of their help.

Fragments, 34

Friendship goes dancing round the world proclaiming to us all to
awake to the praises of a happy life.

Ibid., 52

MENCIUS (MENG TZU)
4th–3rd centuries B.C.

Natural Benevolence

All men have a mind which cannot bear to see the sufferings of
others. . . . When men suddenly see a child about to fall into a
well, they will all experience a feeling of alarm and distress. They
will feel so, not that they may thereon gain the favour of the
child's parents; nor that they may seek the praise of their neighbours and friends; nor from a dislike to the reputation of being
unmoved by such a thing.

Looking at the matter from this case, we may see that to be
without this feeling of distress is not human, and that it is not
human to be without the feeling of shame and dislike, or to be
without the feeling of modesty and complaisance, or to be without the feeling of approving and disapproving. . . .

Since we all have the four principles in ourselves, let us know
to give them all their development and completion, and the issue
will be like that of a fire which has begun to burn, or of a spring
which has begun to find vent. Let them have their full development, and they will suffice to love and protect all within the four

seas; let them be denied that development, and they will not suffice for a man to serve his parents with.

Kung-Sun Cho'w, Book II, 1, 7, trans. James Legge

The Bull Mountain was once covered with lovely trees. But it is
near the capital of a great state. People came with their axes and
choppers; they cut the woods down, and the mountain has lost its
beauty. Yet even so, the day air and the night air came to it, rain
and dew moistened it. Here and there fresh sprouts began to
grow. But soon cattle and sheep came along and browsed on
them, and in the end the mountain became gaunt and bare, as it
is now. And seeing it thus gaunt and bare, people imagine that it
was woodless from the start. Now just as the natural state of the
mountain was quite different from what now appears, so too in
every man (little though they may be apparent) there assuredly
were once feelings of decency and kindliness; and if these good
feelings are no longer there, it is that they have been tampered
with, hewn down with axe and bill. As each day dawns, they are
assailed anew. What chance then has our nature, any more than
that mountain, of keeping its beauty? To us too, as to the mountain, comes the air of day, the air of night. Just at dawn, indeed,
we have for the moment and in a certain degree a mood in which
our promptings and aversions come near to being such as are
proper to men. But something is sure to happen before the morning is over, by which these better feelings are either checked or
else utterly destroyed. And in the end, when they have been
checked again and again, the night air is no longer able to preserve them, and soon our feelings are as near as may be to
those of beasts and birds; so that anyone might make the same
mistake about us as about the mountain, and think that there was
never any good in us from the very start. Yet assuredly our present state of feeling is not what we began with. Truly,

> If rightly tended, no creature but thrives
> If left untended, no creature but pines away.

Kao Tzu, Book VI, 1, 8, trans. Arthur Waley

MARCUS TULLIUS CICERO
106–43 B.C.

The Brotherhood of Man

It is held by the Stoics to be important to understand that nature creates in parents an affection for their children; and parental affection is the source to which we trace the origin of the association of the human race in communities. This cannot but be clear in the first place from the conformation of the body and its members, which by themselves are enough to show that nature's scheme included the procreation of offspring. Yet it could not be consistent that nature should at once intend offspring to be born and make no provision for that offspring when born to be loved and cherished. Even in the lower animals nature's operation can be clearly discerned; when we observe the labour that they spend on bearing and rearing their young, we seem to be listening to the actual voice of nature. Hence as it is manifest that it is natural for us to shrink from pain, so it is clear that we derive from nature herself the impulse to love those to whom we have given birth. From this impulse is developed the sense of mutual attraction which unites human beings as such; this also is bestowed by nature. The mere fact of their common humanity requires that one man should feel another man to be akin to him. . . . (Many animals) do certain actions for the sake of others besides themselves. With human beings this bond of mutual aid is far more intimate. It follows that we are by nature fitted to form unions, societies and states.

Again, they hold that the universe is governed by divine will; it is a city or state of which both men and gods are members, and each one of us is a part of this universe; from which it is a natural consequence that we should prefer the common advantage to our own. For just as the laws set the safety of all above the safety of individuals, so a good, wise and law-abiding man, conscious of his duty to the state, studies the advantage of all more than that of himself or of any single individual. The traitor to his country does not deserve greater reprobation than the man who betrays the common advantage or security for the sake of his own advantage or security. This explains why praise is owed to one who dies

for the commonwealth, because it becomes us to love our country more than ourselves. And as we feel it wicked and inhuman for
men to declare (the saying is usually expressed in a familiar
Greek line) that they care not if, when they themselves are dead,
the universal conflagration ensues, it is undoubtedly true that we
are bound to study the interest of posterity also for its own sake.

De Finibus (About Ends), III, 19, trans. H. Rackham

LUCRETIUS (Titus Lucretius Carus)
c. 96–55 B.C.

On Death

A tree cannot exist high in air, or clouds in the depths of the sea,
as fish cannot live in the fields, or blood flow in wood or sap in
stones. There is a determined and allotted place for the growth
and presence of everything. So mind cannot arise alone without
body or apart from sinews and blood. . . . You must admit, therefore, that when the body has perished there is an end also of the
spirit diffused through it. It is surely crazy to couple a mortal
object with an eternal and suppose that they can work in harmony
and mutually interact. What can be imagined more incongruous,
what more repugnant and discordant, than that a mortal object
and one that is immortal and everlasting should unite to form a
compound and jointly weather the storms that rage about them?

From all this it follows that *death is nothing to us* and no concern of ours, since our tenure of the mind is mortal. In days of old,
we felt no disquiet when the hosts of Carthage poured in to battle on every side—when the whole earth, dizzied by the convul-
sive shock of war, reeled sickeningly under the high ethereal
vault, and between realm and realm the empire of mankind by
land and sea trembled in the balance. So, when we shall be no
more—when the union of body and spirit that engenders us has
been disrupted—to us, who shall then be nothing, nothing by
any hazard will happen any more at all. Nothing will have power
to stir our senses, not though earth be fused with sea and sea
with sky. . . .

If the future holds travail and anguish in store, the self must be in existence, when that time comes, in order to experience it. But from this fate we are redeemed by death, which denies existence to the self that might have suffered these tribulations. Rest assured, therefore, that we have nothing to fear in death. One who no longer is cannot suffer, or differ in any way from one who has never been born, when once this mortal life has been usurped by death the immortal. . . .

The old is always thrust aside to make way for the new, and one thing must be built out of the wreck of another. There is no murky pit of Hell awaiting anyone. There is need of matter, so that later generations may arise; when they have lived out their span, they will all follow you. Bygone generations have taken your road, and those to come will take it no less. So one thing will never cease to spring from another. To none is life given in freehold; to all on lease. Look back at the eternity that passed before we were born, and mark how utterly it counts to us as nothing. This is a mirror that Nature holds up to us, in which we may see the time that shall be after we are dead. Is there anything terrifying in the sight—anything depressing—anything that is not more restful than the soundest sleep?

De Rerum Natura (*On the Nature of the Universe*),
Book III, trans. R. E. Latham

LUCIUS ANNAEUS SENECA
c. 4 B.C.–A.D. 63

On Anger

No man of sense will hate the erring; otherwise he will hate himself. Let him reflect how many times he offends against morality, how many of his acts stand in need of pardon; then he will be angry with himself also. For no just judge will pronounce one sort of judgement in his own case and a different one in the case of others. No one will be found, I say, who is able to acquit himself, and any man who calls himself innocent is thinking more of witnesses than conscience. How much more human to manifest toward wrong-doers a kind and fatherly spirit, not hunting them down but calling them back! If a man has lost his way and is roaming across our fields, it is better to put him upon the right path than to drive him out.

And so the man who does wrong ought to be set right both by admonition and by force, by measures both gentle and harsh, and we should try to make him a better man for his own sake, as well as for the sake of others, stinting, not our reproof, but our anger. For what physician will show anger toward a patient? 'But' you say, 'they are incapable of being reformed, there is nothing pliable in them, nothing that gives room for fair hope.' Then let them be removed from human society if they are bound to make worse all that they touch, and let them, in the only way this is possible, cease to be evil—but let this be done without hatred. For what reason have I for hating a man to whom I am offering the greatest service when I save him from himself? Does a man hate members of his own body when he uses the knife upon them? There is no anger there, but the pitying desire to heal. Mad dogs we knock on the head; the fierce and savage ox we slay; sickly sheep we put to the knife to keep them from infecting the flock; unnatural progeny we destroy. We drown even children who at birth are weakly and abnormal. Yet it is not anger, but reason that separates the harmful from the sound. For the one who administers punishment nothing is so unfitting as anger, since punishment is all the better able to work reform if it is bestowed with judgement. This is the reason Socrates says to his slave: 'I would beat you if I were not angry.' The slave's reproof he postponed to a more rational moment; at the time it was himself he reproved. Will there be any one, pray, who has passion under control, when even Socrates did not dare to trust himself to anger?

Consequently, there is no need that correction be given in anger in order to restrain the erring and the wicked. For since anger is a mental sin, it is not right to correct wrong-doing by doing wrong. . . . 'We have to be angry', you say, 'in order to punish.' What! Think you the law is angry with men it does not know, whom it has never seen, who it hopes will never be? The spirit of the law, therefore, we should make our own—the law which shows not anger but determination. . . . A good judge condemns wrongful deeds, but he does not hate them. 'What then?' you say; 'when the wise man shall have something of this sort to deal with, will not his mind be affected by it, will it not be moved from its usual calm?' I admit that it will; it will experience some slight and superficial emotion. For as Zeno says: 'Even the wise man's mind will keep its scar long after the wound has healed.' He will experience, therefore, certain suggestions and shadows of passion, but from passion itself he will be free. . . .

De Ira (On Anger) 5,15,16

Thoughts on Illness and Death

My ill health had allowed me a long furlough, when suddenly it resumed the attack. . . . I do not know why I should call (my ailment) by its Greek name (asthma); for it is well enough described as 'shortness of breath'. Its attack is of very brief duration, like that of a squall at sea; it usually ends within an hour. Who indeed could breathe his last for long? I have passed through all the ills and dangers of the flesh; but nothing seems to me more troublesome than this. And naturally so; for anything else may be called illness; but this is a sort of continued 'last gasp'. Hence physicians call it 'practising how to die'. For some day the breath will succeed in doing what it has so often essayed. Do you think I am writing this letter in a merry spirit, just because I have escaped? It would be absurd to take delight in such supposed restoration to health, as it would be for a defendant to imagine that he had won his case when he had succeeded in postponing his trial. Yet in the midst of my difficult breathing I never ceased to rest secure in cheerful and brave thoughts.

'What?' I say to myself; 'does death so often test me? Let it do so; I myself have for a long time tested death.' 'When?' you ask. Before I was born. Death is non-existence, and I know already what that means. What was before me will happen again after me. If there is any suffering in this state, there must have been such suffering also in the past, before we entered the light of day. As a matter of fact, however, we felt no discomfort then. And I ask you, would you not say that one was the greatest of fools who believed that a lamp was worse off when it was extinguished than before it was lighted? We mortals also are lighted and extinguished; the period of suffering comes in between, but on either side there is a deep peace.

Epistulae Morales (Moral Epistles), LIV, trans. R. M. Gummere

Euthanasia

You can find men who have gone so far as to profess wisdom and yet maintain that one should not offer violence to one's own life, and hold it accursed for a man to be the means of his own destruction; we should wait, say they, for the end decreed by nature. But one who says this does not see that he is shutting off the path to freedom. The best thing which eternal law ever ordained was that it allowed tó us one entrance into life, but many exits. Must I await the cruelty either of disease or of man, when I can depart through the midst of torture, and shake off my troubles? This is the one reason why we cannot complain of life: it keeps no one against his will. Humanity is well situated, because no man is unhappy except by his own fault. Live, if you so desire; if not, you may return to the place whence you came.

Ibid., LXX

PLINY THE ELDER (Gaius Plinius Secundus)
A.D. 23–79

God in Man

Deus est mortali juvare mortalem. (For mortal to aid mortal—this is God.)

***Natural History*, 11, 5, 18**

PLUTARCH
c. A.D. 46–120

Contentment

A sensible man prays for the better but anticipates the other as well, and, avoiding extremes, makes use of both. Epicurus remarks that 'the man least dependent upon the morrow goes to meet the morrow most cheerfully'; just so do wealth and reputation and power and preferment give the greatest satisfaction to those least apprehensive of their opposites. A vehement desire for these things begets a vehement fear of their not lasting, and this makes the enjoyment of them unstable, like a flickering flame. But if Reason has equipped a man to say to Fortune, without fear or trepidation, 'Very nice, if you bring me something; no harm if you do not', his stoutheartedness, the fact that he does not fear that loss would be intolerable, enables him to enjoy his present blessings with the greatest satisfaction.

On Tranquillity, trans. Moses Hadas

EPICTETUS
1st century A.D.

Disarming the Critic

If anyone tells you that such a person speaks ill of you, do not make excuses about what is said of you, but answer: 'He doth not know my other faults, else he would not have mentioned only these.'

Manual, 33, trans. E. Carter

Do Good Voluntarily

As the sun doth not wait for prayers and incantations to be prevailed on to rise, but immediately shines forth, and is received with universal salutation; so, neither do you wait for applauses and shouts and praises in order to do good; but be a voluntary benefactor, and you will be beloved like the sun.

Ibid., 83

The Claim of Man on Man

A person once brought clothes to a pirate, who had been cast ashore and almost killed by the severity of the weather; then carried him to his house and furnished him with other conveniences. Being reproached by some person for doing good to bad people, 'I have paid this regard', answered he, not to the man, but to human nature.'

Ibid., 104

Citizen of a Democracy

Let no wise man estrange himself from the government of the state; for it is both impious to withdraw from being useful to those that need it, and cowardly to give way to the worthless. For it is foolish to choose rather to be governed ill, than to govern well.
Ibid., 126

Euthanasia

But remember the principal thing: that the door is open. Do not be more fearful than children; but as they, when the play does not please them, say, 'I will play no longer': so do you, in the same case, say, 'I will play no longer', and go; but if you stay, do not complain.
***Discourses*, XXIV, 4**

MARCUS AURELIUS ANTONINUS (EMPEROR)
A.D. 121–180

Disinterested Kindness

One kind of man, when he does a good turn to someone, is forward also to set down the favour to his account. Another is not forward to do this, but still within himself he thinks as though he were a creditor and is conscious of what he has done. A third is in a sense not even conscious of what he has done, but he is like a vine which has borne grapes, and asks nothing more when once it has borne its appropriate fruit. A horse runs, a hound tracks, bees make honey, and a man does good, but doesn't know that he has done it and passes on to a second act, like a vine to bear once more its grapes in due season. You ought then to be one of these who in a way are not aware of what they do.
***Meditations*, V, 6, trans. A. S. L. Farquharson**

Man a Social Animal

As it is with the several members of an organized body, so it is with rational beings who exist separate; the same principle rules, for they also are constituted for a single co-operation. And the perception of this will more strongly strike thy mind, if thou say often to thyself, 'I am a member (*melos*) of the system, of rational beings'. 'But if thou say I am a part (*meros*)', though thou change but one letter of the Greek, thou dost not yet love men from thy heart. Loving-kindness doth not yet delight thee for its own sake: thou still doest it barely as a thing of propriety, and not yet as doing good to thyself.

Ibid., VII, 10, trans. Robert Bridges

Open-mindedness

Suppose a man can convince me of error and bring home to me that I am mistaken in thought or act; I shall be glad to alter, for the truth is what I pursue, and no one was ever injured by the truth, whereas he is injured who continues in his own self-deception and ignorance.

Ibid., VI, 21, trans. A. S. L. Farquharson

Death

Alexander the Great and his stable boy were levelled in death, for they were either taken up into the same life-giving principles of the universe or were scattered without distinction into atoms.

Ibid., VI, 24

A little while and you will be nobody and nowhere, nor will anything which you now behold exist, nor one of those who are now alive. Nature's law is that all things change and turn, and pass away, so that in due order different things may come to be.

Ibid., XI, 1, 21

CELSUS
2nd century A.D.

Celsus's *The True Doctrine*, like most other pagan writings that were unfavourable to Christianity, was destroyed when the Roman Empire became Christian. The substance, however, and probably most of the actual text, has been preserved in *Contra Celsum*, in which Origen, one of the Greek Fathers of the Church, quoted and paraphrased Celsus's arguments at length as a pre-liminary to attacking them. (Ed.)

Anti-intellectualism

Christians usually flee headlong from cultured people, who are not prepared to be deceived; but they trap illiterate folk. . . . Their injunctions are like this. 'Let no one educated, no one wise, no one sensible draw near. For these abilities are thought by us to be evils. But as for anyone ignorant, anyone stupid, anyone une-ducated, anyone who is a child, let him come boldly.' . . . Some of them do not even want to give or receive a reason for what they believe, and use such expressions as 'Do not ask questions; just believe', and 'Thy faith will save thee'. And they say, 'The wis-dom in the world is an evil, and foolishness a good thing'. . . . But why is it bad to have been educated and to have studied the best doctrines, and both to be and to appear intelligent? . . . However, there are among the Christians some moderate, reasonable, and intelligent people, who readily interpret allegorically.

> **The True Doctrine, quoted by Origen,**
> ***Contra Celsum*, VI, 14; III, 44; I, 9, 27**

IBN RUSHD (AVERROËS)
1126–98

Although Averroës was not an unbeliever, he was a considerable sceptic within the context of the Islamic tradition.

On Reason and Religion

Having finished this question Ghazali begins to say that the philosophers deny bodily resurrection. This is a problem which is not found in any of the older philosophers, although resurrection has been mentioned in different religions for at least a thousand years and the philosophers whose theories have come to us are of a more recent date. The first to mention bodily resurrection were the prophets of Israel after Moses, as is evident from the Psalms and many books attributed to the Israelites. Bodily resurrection is also affirmed in the New Testament and attributed by tradition to Jesus. It is a theory of the Sabaeans, whose religion is according to Ibn Hazm the oldest.

But the philosophers in particular, as is only natural, regard this doctrine as most important and believe in it most, and the reason is that it is conducive to an order amongst men on which man's being, as man, depends and through which he can attain the greatest happiness proper to him, for it is a necessity for the existence of the moral and speculative virtues and of the practical sciences in men. They hold namely that man cannot live in this world without the practical sciences, nor in this and the next world without the speculative virtues, and that neither of these categories is perfected or completed without the practical virtues, and that the practical virtues can only become strong through the knowledge and adoration of God by the services prescribed by the laws of the different religions, like offerings and prayers and supplications and other such utterances by which praise is rendered to God, the angels, and the prophets.

In short, the philosophers believe the religious laws are necessary political arts, the principles of which are taken from natural reason and inspiration, especially in what is common to all religions, although religions differ here more or less. The philosophers further hold that one must not object either through a positive or through a negative statement to any of the general religious principles, for instance whether it is obligatory to serve God or not, and still more whether God does or does not exist, and they affirm this also concerning the other religious principles, for instance bliss in the beyond and its possibility; for all religions agree in the acceptance of another existence after death, although they differ in the description of this existence, just as they agree about the knowledge, attributes, and acts of God, although they differ more or less in their utterances about the essence and the acts of the Principle. All religions agree also about the acts conducive to bliss in the next world, although they differ about the determination of these acts.

In short, the religions are, according to the philosophers, obligatory, since they lead towards wisdom in a way universal to all human beings, for philosophy only leads a certain number of intelligent people to the knowledge of happiness, and they therefore have to learn wisdom, whereas religions seek the instruction of the masses generally. Notwithstanding this, we do not find any religion which is not attentive to the special needs of the learned, although it is primarily concerned with the things in which the masses participate. And since the existence of the learned class is only perfected and its full happiness attained by participation with the class of the masses, the general doctrine is also obligatory for the existence and life of this special class, both at the time of their youth and growth (and nobody doubts this), and when they pass on to attain the excellence which is their distinguishing characteristic. For it belongs to the necessary excellence of a man of learning that he should not despise the doctrines in which he has been brought up, and that he should explain them in the fairest way, and that he should understand that the aim of these doctrines lies in their universal character, not in their particularity, and that, if he expresses a doubt concerning the religious principles in which he has been brought up, or explains them in a way contradictory to the prophets and turns away from their path, he merits more than anyone else that the term unbeliever should be applied to him, and he is liable to the penalty for unbelief in the religion in which he has been brought up.

Further, he is under obligation to choose the best religion of his period, even when they are all equally true for him, and he must believe that the best will be abrogated by the introduction of a still better. Therefore the learned who were instructing the people in Alexandria became Muhammedans when Islam reached them, and the learned in the Roman Empire became Christians when the religion of Jesus was introduced there. And nobody doubts that among the Israelites there were many learned men, and this is apparent from the books which are found amongst the Israelites and which are attributed to Solomon. And never has wisdom ceased among the inspired, i.e. the prophets, and therefore it is the truest of all sayings that every prophet is a sage, but not every sage a prophet; the learned, however, are those of whom it is said that they are the heirs of the prophets.

And since in the principles of the demonstrative sciences there are postulates and axioms which are assumed, this must still more be the case for the religions which take their origin in inspiration and reason. Every religion exists through inspiration and is blended with reason. And he who holds that it is possible that there should exist a natural religion based on reason alone must admit that this religion must be less perfect than those which spring from reason and inspiration. And all philosophers agree that the principles of action must be taken on authority, for there is no demonstration for the necessity of action except through the existence of virtues which are realized through moral actions and through practice.

**From *Tahajfut al-tahajfut*
(*The Incoherence of Incoherence*)**

MICHEL EYQUEM DE MONTAIGNE
1533–1592

Miracles and Witchcraft

I have seen the birth of many miracles in my time. . . . Now the first persons that are possessed of the beginning of this marvellous affair, when they start telling their tale, learn by the resistance they meet with where the difficulty of persuasion lies, and to caulk up that place with some piece of falsehood. Besides that, *insita hominibus libidine alendi de industria rumores* (men having a natural desire to nourish reports), we naturally make it a point of conscience to restore what has been lent us with something of our own added by way of interest. First the private error creates the public error, and afterwards, in its turn, the public error promotes the private error. Thus, all this vast fabric goes forming and piling itself up from hand to hand, so that the remotest witness knows more about it than those who were nearest, and the last informed is better persuaded than the first. . . .

The witches of my neighbourhood go in peril of their lives at the instance of every new author who arrives to give body to their fantasies. . . . I am plain and heavy, and stick to the solid and the probable, avoiding those ancient reproaches, *majorem fidem homines adhibent iis, quae non intelligunt—cupidine humani ingenii, libentius obscura creduntur* (men are most apt to believe what they least understand: and, through the lust of human wit, obscure things are more easily credited). I see very well that men get angry, and that I am forbidden to doubt upon pain of execrable injuries. A new way of persuading! Thank God, I am not to be cuffed into belief. . . . He who would establish his proposition by authority and huffing shows that reason is of small account in it. . . .

I have my ears battered with a thousand such flimflams as these: 'Three persons saw him such a day in the east; three, the next day in the west; at such an hour, in such a place, and in such habit.' In sooth I should not believe myself in such a matter. How much more natural and likely do I find it that two men should lie, than that one man in twelve hours' time should fly with the wind from the east to the west! How much more natural that our understanding should be carried from its place by the volubility of our disordered minds, than that one of us should be carried by a strange spirit upon a broomstaff, flesh and bones as we are, up the shaft of a chimney? Let us not look for external unknown illusions, we who are perpetually agitated with illusions within ourselves. I think we are justified in disbelieving a miracle so long as, by non-miraculous means, one may elude its verification as such. I am of St. Augustine's opinion that in things hard to prove and dangerous to believe it is better to lean towards doubt than towards assurance. . . .

As to the objections and arguments with which honest men have confronted me, both in this matter and often in others, I have met with none that have convinced me, and that have not admitted a more likely interpretation than theirs. The proofs and reasons founded upon experience and fact—these, it is true, I do not go about to untie. They have no end to get hold of: I often cut them, as Alexander did the Gordian knot. After all, it is putting a very high value on one's conjectures to roast a man alive on the strength of them.

Essay 'Of Cripples' (1580), trans. Gerald Builett

Of Mortal Contentment

When Philosophers blazon and display the Hierarchy of their gods, and to the utmost of their skill endevour to distinguish their aliances, their charges, and their powers. I cannot believe they speake in good earnest when Plato decyphreth unto us the orchard of Pluto, and the commodities or corporall paines, which even after the ruine and consumption of our body, waite for us, and applyeth them to the apprehension or feeling we have in this life.

> Secreti celant cones, et myrtia circum
> Sylva tegit, curae non ipsa in morte relinquunt.
> **Virgil,** *Aeneid,* **VI, 44.**

> Them paths aside conceale, a mirtle grove
> Shades them round; cares in death doe not remove.

When Mahomet promiseth unto his followers a paradise all tapistred, adorned with gold and precious stones, peopled with exceeding beauteous damsels, stored with wines and singular cates,* I well perceive they are but scoffers, which sute and apply themselves unto our foolishnesse, thereby to enhonny and allure us to these opinions and hopes fitting our mortall appetite. Even so are some of our men falne into like errours by promising unto themselves after their resurrection a terrestriall and temporall like, accompanied with al sorts of pleasures and wordly commodities. Shall we thinke that Plato, who had so heavenly conceptions, and was so well acquainted with Divinity, as of most he purchased the surname of Divine, was ever of opinion, that man (this seely and wretched creature man) had any one thing in him, which might in any sort be applied, and suted to this imcomprehensible and unspeakable power? or ever imagined, that our languishing hold-fasts were capable, or the vertue of our understanding of force, to participate or be partakers, either of the blessednesse, or eternall punishment? He ought in the bhalfe of humane reason be answered: If the pleasures, thou promisest us in the other life, are such as I have felt here below, they have nothing in them common with infinity. If all my five naturall senses were even surcharged with joy and gladnesse, and my soule possessed with all the contents and delights, it could possibly desire or hope for (and we know what it either can wish or hope for) yet were [it] nothing. If there bee any thing that is mine, then is there nothing that is Divine; if it be nothing else, but what may appertaine unto this our present condition, it may not be ac-

---

*Food

counted of. *All mortall mens contentment is mortall.* The acknowledging of our parents, of our children, of our friends, if it cannot touch, move or tickle us in the other world, if we still take hold of such a pleasure, we continue in Terrestrial and transitorie commodities. We can not worthily conceive of these high, mysterious, and divine promises; if wee can but in any sort conceive them, and so imagine them aright; they must be thought to be inimaginable, unspeakable and incomprehensible, and absolutely and perfectly other than those of our miserable experience.

from *An Apology to Raymond Sebond*,
trans. Florio (17th c. ?)

GIORDANO BRUNO
1548–1600

Of the Oneness of the Universe

In the fifth dialogue, which treats especially of the One, the foundation of the edifice, of the natural and divine knowledge, is completed. There, in the first place, the conception of the coincidence of matter and form, of potency and act, is established, in such a way, that 'being', though logically divided into that which is, and that which can be, is really indivisible, indistinct, and one; and that it is at the same time, infinite, immobile, and indivisible, and without difference of part and whole, principle and principled. Second, that in that (One), the century is not different from the year, the year from the moment, the span from the furlong, the furlong from the mile; and in its nature, this and that other specific being is not other and other; and therefore there is no number in the universe, and therefore the universe is one. Third, that the point is not different from the body in the Infinite: because act and potency are not different things, and therefore, the point can run on at length, the line be extended in width, and the surface, in depth; the first is long, the second is wide, and the third is deep; and since everything is long, wide, and deep (consequently) they are one and the same, and the universe is all center and all circumference. Fourth, from the fact that Jove (as they call him) is found to be more intimately in all, that the form of all can be imagined to be there (because he is the essence, through which all that is, has being; and since he is in all totally, everything has in itself the all, more intimately than its proper form), it is inferred that everything is in everything and, consequently, all is one. Fifth, answer is made to the doubt that demands to know: why all particular things change, and why the particular 'matters', in order to receive one and another being, are forced to new and other forms; and it is shown how there is unity in multiplicity, and multiplicity in unity; and how being has many modes, and a multiple unity, and finally, that it is one in substance and truth. Sixth, inference is made concerning the derivation of that difference of particular things, and of that number of particular matters, and it is made explicit, that they are not being, but of being and about being. Seventh, it is marked that he who has found that one, that is to say, the reason of this unity, has found that key, without which it is impossible to enter into the true contemplation of nature. Eighth, with renewed contemplation, answer is made, that the One, the Infinite, the Being, and that which is in all, is throughout all, the selfsame, everywhere; just as the indivisible infinite multitude, not being 'number,' coincides with unity. Ninth, how, in the Infinite, there are no parts, parts being reserved for the unfolded universe; where, however, all that we see of diversity and difference are nothing but diverse and different aspects of the same Substance. Tenth, how, in the two extremes that are spoken of in the extremity of the ladder of nature, not two principles must be considered, but one; not two beings, but one; not two contrary and diverse principles, but one; concordant and identical. In it, height is depth; the abyss is the inaccessible light; obscurity is clarity; the great is the small; the confused is the distinct; strife is friendship; the divided is the indivisible; the atom is immense; and conversely. Eleventh, how, and in what way, certain geometrical denominations, like the point and the unity, are understood, in order to promote the contemplation of Being and the One; and how, they are not sufficient, of themselves, to express that. For which reason, Pythagoras, Parmenides, and Plato must not be rashly interpreted, in accordance with the pedantic censure of Aristotle. Twelfth, from this: that Substance and being are distinct from quantity, from measure, and from number, it is inferred that it [Substance] is one and indivisible in all and in whatever thing that exists. Thirteenth, the signs and the proofs, through which it is shown, that contraries truly coincide, are reported; that they are derived from one principle, and that they are one in reality and Substance; all of which, is concluded to be true, physically, after having been shown to be true mathematically.

Behold then, most illustrious gentleman, from what point it is necessary to leave, in order to enter into that most special and most appropriate knowledge of things. Here, as in its proper seeds, is contained, and it implied, the multitude of conclusions concerning natural science. From here is derived the structure, the disposition, and the order of the speculative sciences. Without this introduction, it is vain to attempt, to begin, and to enter into that knowledge. Take then, willingly, this principle, this one, this fountain, this beginning, so that its seeds and its progeny may become stimulated to go out into the light of day; so that its rivulets, and many streams, may become diffused—multiplying their number successively, and disposing its members, each time further and further—so that, finally, with the ceasing of the night, with its somnolent veil and obscure mantel, the mighty Titan—parent of the divine muses, adorned by his family, and surrounded by his eternal court—brings forth the triumphal carriage from the red bosom of this gallant Aurora (after banishing the nocturnal torches), adorning the world with a new day. Farewell.

from *Dialogue discussing*
'Concerning the Cause, Principle, and One'

BENEDICT (Baruch) SPINOZA
1632–1677

The Nature of God*

Further, I should like to remark here that while we are speaking philosophically we must not use the modes of expression of the-

---

*Spinoza referred frequently and reverently to 'God,' but the term to him was no more than a synonym for Nature—an impersonal Force or Being to whom it was meaningless to apply such concepts as 'good' or 'loving'. In the words of Santayana (introduction to Everyman edition), 'When we catch the philosophical intention behind this pious language, we perceive that Spinoza is sounding the very depths of rationalism.' Spinoza was execrated as an atheist during his lifetime, and was excommunicated by the Amsterdam synagogue. (Ed.)

ology. For theology has usually, and not without reason, represented God as a perfect man; therefore it is quite appropriate in theology that it should be said that God desires something, that God is affected with weariness at the deeds of the ungodly, and with pleasure at those of the pious. But in philosophy, where we clearly understand that to apply to God the attributes which make a man perfect, is as bad as to want to apply to a man those which make perfect an elephant or an ass, these and similar words have no place; and we cannot use them here without thoroughly confusing our conceptions.

Letter to van Blyenbergh (1665), trans. A. Wolf

Virtue, Freedom and Servitude

Beatitudo non est virtutis praemium, sed ipsa virtus. (Blessedness is not the reward of virtue, but virtue itself.)

***Ethics* (1674), V, 42**

Omnia praeclara tam difficilia quam rara sunt. (All excellent things are as difficult as they are rare.)

Ibid., V. 42, note

A man's inability to moderate and control his passions I call servitude. . . . The common vulgar opinion seems to be quite otherwise. For most people seem to believe that they are free just in so far as they may obey their lusts, and that they renounce their rights in so far as they are constrained to live according to the precepts of divine law. Wherefore they believe that Piety and Religion (that is to live according to Reason and the knowledge of God) and whatever else regards fortitude of mind, are burdens which they hope to get rid of at death, when they will receive the reward of their servitude, that is of their piety and religion. And it is not only by this hope, but also and principally by the fear of terrible punishments after death, that they are induced to live by the precepts of divine law as far as their meagre and impotent spirit will carry them. And had they not this hope and fear, but believed rather that the mind perished with the body, and would not survive it when they die miserably worn out by the burden of their piety, they would surely return to their inborn disposition, and wish to govern all things by their lusts, submitting everything to the government of fortune rather than to themselves. All this appears to me no less absurd than that a man, because he did not believe that he could keep his body alive for ever by wholesome diet, should stuff himself with poisons and deadly food: or, deeming his mind not to be eternal and immortal, should therefore wish to be mad, and live without reason.

Ibid., IV (preface), V. 41 (note), trans. Robert Bridges

JEAN MESLIER
1664–1729

The Abbé Meslier was appointed curué of Etrépigny, in Champagne, at the age of twenty-five, and remained there until his death forty years later. As a vigorous campaigner against the social injustices of his day, he was in frequent conflict with ecclesiastical and civil authority. But this did not prepare his parishioners for the discovery, after his death, of three signed copies of a manuscript entitled *Mon Testament*, which contained a scathing denunciation of Christianity. 'I did not', said the Abbé, 'wish to burn until after my death.'

The manuscript was frequently copied, and apparently fairly widely circulated, in the years that followed; but no part of it was printed until 1762, when Voltaire edited an *Extrait*, with a short life of the author. ('He has', said Voltaire in a letter to Hevétius, 'the style of a cart-horse, but he kicks to some purpose.') The *Extrait* was reprinted several times, often in the same volume as d'Holbach's *Bon Sens*, and the latter became erroneously attributed to Meslier. The full text of Meslier's *Testament* was not printed until 1861 (Amsterdam, 3 vols.).

The extracts here quoted have been freely translated and abridged. (Ed.)

The Abbé's Apology to his Flock

It was not from cupidity that I was led to adopt a profession so opposed to my convictions: I obeyed my parents. I would have enlightened you sooner, if I could have done so with safety. You are my witness that I have never exacted the fees that attach to my office as curé. I discouraged you from bigotry, and I spoke to you as seldom as possible of our wretched dogmas. I had to carry out the duties of my office, but how I suffered when I had to preach to you those pious lies that I detest in my heart! What remorse your credulity caused me! A thousand times I was on the point of breaking out publicly and opening your eyes, but a fear stronger than myself held me back, and forced me to keep silence until my death.

Preface to *Mon Testament*, quoted by Voltaire in a letter to the Comte d'Argental, February 1762, trans. M. K.

The Credibility of the Gospels

It is no use saying that the Gospel stories have always been regarded as holy and sacred, and that they have been faithfully preserved without any tampering. It was common practice among the writers who copied these stories to add, delete, or alter the text as seemed good to them. The Christians themselves cannot deny this; for St. Jerome (translator of the Vulgate) said explicitly in many places in his Prologues that the text had been corrupted and falsified, having already been through the hands of many people who added and cut out as they pleased; with the result, as he said, that there were as many different readings as there were different texts.

The heretics of our time (i.e. the Protestants) reject as apocryphal many books that Roman Catholics regard as holy and sacred, such as those of Tobit, Judith, Esther, Baruch, the Wisdom of Solomon, Ecclesiasticus and I and II Maccabees; to which uncertain and doubtful books one could add several attributed to the apostles, for example the Acts of St. Thomas, his journey, his Gospel and his Apocalypse; the Gospel of St. Bartholomew, of St. Peter, and of the Apostles; the Book of the Judgment, the Book of the Childhood of the Saviour, and many others of the same kidney, which are all rejected as aprocryphal by Roman Catholics.

Which all goes to show that there is no firm basis for the authority claimed for the canonical Gospels. Those who say that these books are divinely inspired must admit that they know this by faith alone, faith which makes it impossible for them to believe otherwise. But how can faith (or in other words, blind credulity) establish the authority of the books that are the ground of this faith? What folly is this?

***Extrait du Testament de J. Meslier*, by Voltaire (1762), Chap. 1, 2**

The Incarnation

The main purpose, we are told, which God had in mind when he sent his son down to earth in human form, was to take away the sins of the world, and to destroy the works of the devil. Jesus promised frequently that he would deliver the world from sin. Was there ever a falser prophecy?—as the present century bears witness. It is said that Jesus came to save mankind. Mankind, indeed! If an army of a hundred thousand soldiers is made captive, and some ten or a dozen men are ransomed, one does not say that the army has been ransomed. What are we to think of a God who comes to be crucified and to die to save the world, and who leaves so many nations to damnation?

Ibid., III: V, 2

Envoi

On what do the Christians pride themselves? Their moral code? It is the same at bottom as that of all religions: but cruel dogmas have sprung from it and taught men to persecute. Their miracles? But what people have not had their miraculous stories, and what wise men have not rejected them? Their prophecies? Have they not been falsified? Their conduct? Is it not often infamous? The establishment of their religion? But has it not sprung from fanaticism and been sustained by intrigue? Their doctrine? But is it not the height of absurdity? I hope, my friends, that I have given you a sufficient protection against these follies.

Ibid., VI, 2

FRANÇOIS MARIE AROUET (VOLTAIRE)
1694–1778

Toleration

One does not need great art and skilful eloquence to prove that Christians ought to tolerate each other—nay, even to regard all men as brothers. Why, you say, is the Turk, the Chinese, or the Jew my brother? Assuredly; are we not all children of the same father, creatures of the same God?

But these people despise us and treat us as idolaters. Very well; I will tell them they are quite wrong. It seems to me that I might astonish, at least, the stubborn pride of a Mohammedan or a Buddhist priest if I spoke to them somewhat as follows:

This little globe, which is but a point, travels in space like many other globes; we are lost in the immensity. Man, about five feet high, is certainly a small thing in the universe. One of these imperceptible beings says to some of his neighbours, in Arabia or South Africa: 'Listen to me, for the God of all these worlds has enlightened me. There are nine hundred million little ants like us on the earth, but my ant-hole alone is dear to God. All the others are eternally reprobated by him. Mine alone will be happy.'

They would then interrupt me, and ask who was the fool that talked all this nonsense. I should be obliged to tell them that it was themselves. I would then try to appease them, which would be difficult.

I would next address myself to the Christians, and would venture to say to, for instance, a Dominican friar—an inquisitor of the faith: 'Brother, you are aware that each province in Italy has its own dialect, and that people do not speak at Venice and Bergamo as they do at Florence. The academy of La Crusca has fixed the language. Its dictionary is a rule that has to be followed, and the grammar of Matei is an infallible guide. But do you think that the consul of the Academy, or Matei in his absence, could in conscience cut out the tongues of all the Venetians and the Bergamese who persisted in speaking their own dialect?'

The inquisitor replies: 'The two cases are very different. In our case it is a question of your eternal salvation. It is for your good that the heads of the Inquisition direct that you shall be seized on the information of any one person, however infamous or criminal; that you shall have no advocate to defend you; that the name of your accuser shall not be made known to you; that the inquisitor shall promise you pardon and then condemn you; and that you shall then be subjected to five kinds of torture, and afterwards either flogged or sent to the galleys or ceremoniously burned. On this Father Ivonet, Doctor Cuchalon, Zanchinus, Campegius, Royas, Felinus, Gomarus, Diabarus and Gemelinus are explicit, and this pious practice admits of no exception.'

I would take the liberty of replying: 'Brother, possibly you are right. I am convinced that you wish to do me good. But could I not be saved without all that?'

It is true that these absurd horrors do not stain the face of the earth every day; but they have often done so, and the record of them would make up a volume much longer than the gospels which condemn them. Not only is it cruel to persecute, in this brief life, those who differ from us, but I am not sure if it is not too bold to declare that they are damned eternally. It seems to me that it is not the place of the atoms of a moment, such as we are, thus to anticipate the decrees of the Creator. Far be it from me to question the principle, 'Out of the Church there is no salvation.' I respect it, and all that it teaches; but do we really know all the ways of God, and the full range of his mercies? May we not hope in him as much as fear him? Is it not enough to be loyal to the Church? Must each individual usurp the rights of the Deity, and decide, before he does, the eternal lot of all men?

When we wear mourning for a king of Sweden, Denmark, England, or Prussia, do we say that we wear mourning for one who burns eternally in hell? There are in Europe forty million people who are not of the Church of Rome. Shall we say to each of them: 'Sir, seeing that you are infallibly damned, I will neither eat, nor deal, nor speak with you'?

What ambassador of France, presented in audience to the Sultan, would say in the depths of his heart: 'His Highness will undoubtedly burn for all eternity because he has been circumcised'? If he really believed that the Sultan is the mortal enemy of God, the object of his vengeance, could he speak to him? Ought he to be sent to him? With whom could we trade? What duty of civil life could we ever fulfil if we were really convinced that we were dealing with damned souls?

Followers of a merciful God, if you were cruel at heart; if, in worshipping him whose whole law consisted in loving one's neighbour as oneself, you have burdened this pure and holy law with sophistry and unintelligible disputes; . . . if you had attached eternal torment to the omission of a few words or ceremonies that other peoples could not know, I should say to you:

'Transport yourselves with me to the day on which all men will be judged, when God will deal with each according to his works. I see the dead of former ages and of our own stand in his presence. Are you sure that our Creator and Father will say to the wise and virtuous Confucius, to the lawgiver Solon, to Pythagoras, to Zaleucus, to Socrates, to Plato, to the divine Antonines, to the good Trajan, to Titus, the delight of the human race, to Epictetus and to so many other model men: "Go, monsters, go and submit to a chastisement infinite in its intensity and duration; your torment shall be as eternal as I. And you, my beloved Jean Chatel, Ravaillac, Damiens, Cartouche, etc. (assassins in the cause of the Church), who have died with the prescribed formulae, come and share my empire and felicity for ever." '

You shrink with horror from such sentiments; and, now that they have passed my lips, I have no more to say to you.

A Treatise on Toleration (1763), trans. Joseph McCabe

Christianized Rome

(Voltaire writes in the character of an imaginary Count de Corbera, 'a Roman gentleman of an ancient and transplanted family, one who cherishes his venerable country, bemoans her condition, and has left his heart in her Capitol'.)

Romans, listen to your fellow citizen; listen to Rome and your ancient valour. . . . When I travelled among you . . . (I marvelled what had) so greatly changed your soil, your fortunes, and your spirit. Whence comes it . . . that from Montefiascone to Viterbo, and in the whole region through which the Appian way still leads to Naples, a vast desert has replaced the smiling land that was once covered with palaces, gardens, harvests, and countless numbers of citizens? I sought the Forum Romanum of Trajan, that square once paved with reticulated marble, surrounded by a colonnaded peristyle and adorned with a hundred statues; and what I found was the Campo Vacino, the cattle-market, a market of lean and milkless cows. And I asked myself: Where are those two million Romans who once peopled this capital? . . . Setting aside Jews, priests, and foreigners, Rome cannot have one hundred thousand inhabitants. I asked of them: Whose is this splendid building that I see, girt about with ruins? It belongs to the monks, they said. Here once was the house of Augustus; there Cicero dwelt, and there Pompey. On their ruins have arisen convents.

I wept, Romans; and I think highly enough of you to believe that you weep with me.

Epistle to the Romans (1768), trans. Joseph McCabe

The Prime Architect

Dondindac: Before receiving your instruction, I must tell you what happened to me one day. I had just had a closet built at the end of my garden. I heard a mole arguing with a cockchafer: 'Here's a fine structure', said the mole; 'it must have been a very powerful mole who did this work.' 'You're joking', said the cockchafer; 'it's a cockchafer full of genius who is the architect of this building.' From that moment I resolved never to argue.

from *Philosophical Dictionary* (1764)

Conciles: Councils

All councils are undoubtedly infallible: for they are composed of men. It is impossible for passions, intrigues, the lust for dispute, hatred, jealousy, prejudice, ignorance ever to reign in these assemblies.

But why, it will be asked, have so many councils contradicted each other? It is to try our faith. Each was in the right in its turn.

Roman Catholics now believe only in councils approved by the Vatican; and the Greek Catholics believe only in those approved in Constantinople. Protestants deride them both. Thus everybody should be satisfied.

I shall refer here only to the great councils; the small ones are not worth the trouble.

The first one was that of Nicaea. It was assembled in 325 of the common era, after Constantine had written and sent by the hand of Ozius this noble letter to the rather confused clergy of Alexandria: 'You are quarrelling about something very trivial. These subtleties are unworthy of sensible people.' The thing was to determine whether Jesus was created or uncreated. This has nothing to do with morality, which is the essential point. Whether Jesus was in time or before time, we must none the less be good. After many altercations it was finally decided that the son was as old as the father, and consubstantial with the father. This decision is hardly comprehensible, but it is all the more sublime on that account. Seventeen bishops protested against the decree, and an ancient chronicle of Alexandria, preserved at Oxford, says that 2,000 priests also protested; but prelates pay little attention to simple priests, who are usually poor. Be that as it may, there was no question whatever of the trinity in this first council. The formula reads: 'We believe Jesus consubstantial with the father, god of god, light of light, begotten and not made; we also believe in the holy ghost.' The holy ghost, it must be admitted, was treated pretty off-handedly.

It is reported in the supplement of the council of Nicaea that the fathers, being very perplexed to know which were the cryphal or apocryphal books of the Old and New Testaments, put them all pell-mell on an altar, and the books to be rejected fell to the ground. It is a pity that this elegant procedure has not survived.

Ibid.

DAVID HUME
1711–1776

The Argument from Design

(A discussion is in progress between Cleanthes, a theistic philosopher, Philo, a sceptic, and Demea, an orthodox Christian.)

Not to lose any time in circumlocutions, said Cleanthes . . . I shall briefly explain how I conceive this matter. Look round the world: Contemplate the whole and every part of it: You will find it to be nothing but one great machine, subdivided into an infinite number of lesser machines, which again admit of subdivisions, to a degree beyond what human senses and faculties can trace and explain. All these various machines, and even their most minute parts, are adjusted to each other with an accuracy, which ravishes into admiration all men, who have ever contemplated them. The curious adapting of means to ends, throughout all nature, resembles exactly, though it much exceeds, the productions of human contrivance; of human design, thought, wisdom, and intelligence. Since therefore the effects resemble each other, we are led to infer, by all the rules of analogy, that the causes also resemble; and that the Author of nature is somewhat similar to the mind of man; though possessed of much larger faculties proportioned to the grandeur of the work, which he has executed. By this argument a posteriori, and by this argument alone, we do prove at once the existence of a Deity, and his similarity to human mind and intelligence. . . .

That I chiefly scruple in this subject, said Philo, is not so much, that all religious arguments are by Cleanthes reduced to experience, as that they appear not to be even the most certain and irrefragable of that inferior kind. That a stone will fall, that fire will burn, that the earth has solidity, we have observed a thousand and a thousand times; and when any new instance of this nature is presented, we draw without hesitation the accustomed inference. The exact similarity of the cases gives us a perfect assurance of a similar event; and a stronger evidence is never desired nor sought after. But wherever you depart, in the least, from the similarity of the cases, you diminish proportionably the evidence; and may at last bring it to a very weak analogy, which is confessedly liable to error and uncertainty. After having experienced the circulation of the blood in human creatures, we make no doubt that it takes place in Titius and Maevius: But from its circulation in frogs and fishes, it is only a presumption, though a strong one, from analogy, that it takes place in men and other animals. The analogical reasoning is much weaker, when we infer the circulation of the sap in vegetables from our experience that the blood circulates in animals; and those, who hastily followed that imperfect analogy, are found, by more accurate experiments, to have been mistaken.

If we see a house, Cleanthes, we conclude, with the greatest certainty, that it had an architect or builder; because this is precisely that species of effect, which we have experienced to proceed from that species of cause. But surely you will not affirm, that the universe bears such a resemblance to a house, that we can with the same certainty infer a similar cause, or that the analogy is here entire and perfect. The dissimilitude is so striking, that the utmost you can here pretend to is a guess, a conjecture, a presumption concerning a similar cause; and how that pretension will be received in the world, I leave you to consider. . . .

But to show you still more inconveniences, continued Philo, in your anthropomorphism; please to take a new survey of your principles. *Like effects prove like causes*. This is the experimental argument. . . . Now it is certain that the liker the effects are, which are seen, and the liker the causes, which are inferred, the stronger is the argument. Every departure on either side diminishes the probability, and renders the experiment less conclusive. You cannot doubt of this principle: Neither ought you to reject its consequences. . . .

Now Cleanthes, said Philo, with an air of alacrity and triumph, mark the consequences. First, By this method of reasoning, you renounce all claim to infinity in any of the attributes of the Deity. For as the cause ought only to be proportioned to the effect, and the effect, so far as it falls under our cognisance, is not infinite; what pretensions have we, upon your suppositions, to ascribe that attribute to the divine Being? . . .

Secondly, You have no reason, on your theory, for ascribing perfection to the Deity, even in his finite capacity; or for supposing him free from every error, mistake, or incoherence in his undertakings. . . .

And what shadow of an argument, continued Philo, can you produce, from your hypothesis, to prove the unity of the Deity? A great number of men join in building a house or ship, in rearing a city, in framing a commonwealth: Why may not several Deities combine in contriving and framing a world? This is only so much greater similarity to human affairs. . . .

But farther, Cleanthes; men are mortal, and renew their species by generation; and this is common to all living creatures. The two great sexes of male and female, says Milton, animate the world. Why must this circumstance, so universal, so essential, be excluded from those numerous and limited Deities? Behold then the theogony of ancient times brought back upon us. . . .

In a word, Cleanthes, a man, who follows your hypothesis, is able, perhaps, to assert, or conjecture, that the universe, sometime, arose from something like design: But beyond that position he cannot ascertain one single circumstance, and is left afterwards to fix every point of his theology by the utmost licence of fancy and hypothesis. This world, for aught he knows, is very faulty and imperfect, compared to a superior standard; and was only the first rude essay of some infant Deity, who afterwards abandoned it, ashamed of his lame performance; it is the work only of some dependent, inferior Deity; and is the object of derision to his superiors: it is the production of old age and dotage in some superannuated Deity; and ever since his death, has run on at adventures, from the first impulse and active force, which it received from him. ... You justly give signs of horror, Demea, at these strange suppositions: But these, and a thousand more of the same kind, are Cleanthes's suppositions, not mine. From the moment the attributes of the Deity are supposed finite, all these have place. ...

These suppositions I absolutely disown, cried Cleanthes: They strike me, however, with no horror; especially, when proposed in that rambling way in which they drop from you. On the contrary, they give me pleasure, when I see, that, by the utmost indulgence of your imagination, you never get rid of the hypothesis of design in the universe; but are obliged, at every turn, to have recourse to it. To this concession I adhere steadily; and this I regard as a sufficient foundation for religion.

(But) there occurs to me another hypothesis (continued Philo) which must acquire an air of probability from the method of reasoning so much insisted on by Cleanthes. ... If we survey the universe, so far as it falls under our knowledge, it bears a great resemblance to an animal or organized body, and seems actuated with a like principle of life and motion. A continual circulation of matter in it produces no disorder: A continual waste in every part is incessantly repaired: The closest sympathy is perceived throughout the entire system: And each part or member, in performing its proper offices, operates both to its own preservation and to that of the whole. The world, therefore, I infer, is an animal, and the Deity is the SOUL of the world, actuating it, and actuated by it. ...

This theory, I own, replied Cleanthes, has never before occurred to me, though a pretty natural one; and I cannot readily upon so short an examination and reflection, deliver any opinion with regard to it. You are very scrupulous, indeed, said Philo; were I to examine any system of yours, I should not have acted with half that caution and reserve, in starting objections and difficulties to it. However, if any thing occur to you, you will oblige us by proposing it.

Why then, replied Cleanthes, it seems to me that, though the world does in many circumstances, resemble an animal body; yet is the analogy also defective in many circumstances, the most material: No organs of sense; no seat of thought or reason; no one precise origin of motion and action. In short, it seems to bear a stronger resemblance to a vegetable than to an animal; and your inference would be so far inconclusive in favour of the soul of the world. . . .

But here, continued Philo, there strikes me, all on a sudden, a new idea. . . . If the universe bears a greater likeness to animal bodies and to vegetables, than to the works of human art, it is more probable that its cause resembles the cause of the former than that of the latter, and its origin ought rather to be ascribed to generation or vegetation than to reason or design. . . .

Pray open up this argument a little farther, said Demea. For I do not rightly apprehend it, in that concise manner in which you have expressed it.

Our friend, Cleanthes, replied Philo, as you have heard, asserts, that . . . the world . . . resembles the works of human contrivance: Therefore its cause must also resemble that of the other. . . . But I affirm, that . . . the world plainly resembles more an animal or a vegetable, than it does a watch or a knitting-loom. Its cause, therefore, it is more probable, resembles the cause of the former. The cause of the former is generation or vegetation. The cause, therefore, of the world, we may infer to be some thing similar or analogous to generation or vegetation.

But how is it conceivable, said Demea, that the world can arise from any thing similar to vegetation or generation?

Very easily, replied Philo. In like manner as a tree sheds its seed into the neighbouring fields, and produces other trees; so the great vegetable, the world, or this planetary system, produces within itself certain seeds, which being scattered into the surrounding chaos, vegetate into new worlds. A comet, for instance, is the seed of a world. . . .

Or if, for the sake of variety (for I see no other advantage), we should suppose this world to be an animal; a comet is the egg of this animal; and in like manner as an ostrich lays its egg in the sand, which, without any farther care, hatches the egg, and produces a new animal; so . . .

I understand you, says Demea: But what wild, arbitrary suppositions are these? What data have you for such extraordinary conclusions? And is the slight, imaginary resemblance of the world to a vegetable or an animal sufficient to establish the same inference with regard to both? Objects, which are in general so widely different; ought they to be a standard for each other?

Right, cries Philo: This is the topic on which I have all along insisted. I have still asserted, that we have no data to establish any system of cosmogony. Our experience, so imperfect in itself, and so limited both in extent and duration, can afford us no probable conjecture concerning the whole of things. But if we must needs fix on some hypothesis; by what rule, pray, ought we to determine our choice? Is there any other rule than the greater similarity of the objects compared? And does not a plant or an animal, which springs from vegetation or generation, bear a stronger resemblance to the world, than does any artificial machine, which arises from reason and design? . . .

I must confess, Philo, replied Cleanthes, that of all men living, the task which you have undertaken, of raising doubts and objections, suits you best, and seems, in a manner, natural and unavoidable to you. So great is your fertility of invention, that I am not ashamed to acknowledge myself unable, in a sudden, to solve regularly such out-of-the-way difficulties as you incessantly start upon me: Though I clearly see, in general, their fallacy and error; . . . while you must be sensible, that common sense and reason is entirely against you, and that such whimsies, as you have delivered, may puzzle, but never can convince us.

Dialogues concerning Natural Religion (1779), Parts II, V, VI, VII

DENIS DIDEROT
1713–1784

Damnation

DAMNATION (Theol.). Eternal punishment of hell. The dogma of damnation or eternal punishment is clearly revealed in Scripture. So it is useless for us to reason about such matters as whether

a finite being can do an infinite wrong to God; whether the inflic-
tion of unending torment is more contrary to God's goodness than
it is consonant with his justice; whether, since God has been
pleased to attach an infinite reward to virtue, it follows by necessity that he must attach an infinite penalty to sin. Instead of
embroiling ourselves in captious reasonings that may shake an
unstable faith, let us rather submit ourselves to the authority of
Holy Scripture and the decisions of the Church, and work out our
salvation in fear and trembling; remembering always that the mag-
nitude of an offence must inevitably be proportionate to the dignity
of the Offended, and inversely proportionate to that of the offender.
And what must be the enormity of our disobedience, since that of
Adam could be effaced only by the blood of the Son of God?

Encyclopédie, Vol. IV (1754), trans. M. K.

Creating a Fantasy

Philosophical thought. A man had been betrayed by his children,
by his wife, and by his friends; some disloyal partners had ruined
his fortune, and had plunged him into poverty. Pervaded with a
profound hatred and contempt for the human race, he left society
and took refuge alone in a cave. There, pressing his fists into his
eyes, and contemplating a revenge proportional to his griev-
ances, he said: 'Evil people! What shall I do to punish them for
their injustice and to make them all as unhappy as they deserve?
Ah! if it were possible to imagine it—to intoxicate them with a
great fantasy to which they would attach more importance than to
their lives, and about which they would never be able to agree!'

Instantly he rushed out of the cave, shouting, 'God! God!'
Echoes without number repeated around him, 'God! God!' This
fearful name was carried from pole to pole, and heard everywhere
with astonishment. At first men prostrated themselves, then they
got up again, asked each other, argued with each other, became
bitter, cursed each other, hated each other, cut each other's
throats, and the fatal wish of the misanthropist was fulfilled. For
such has been in the past, such will be in the future, the story of
a being at all times equally important and incomprehensible.

from Addition to Philosophical Thoughts
(*Correspondance Littéraire*) (1763)

PAUL HENRI THIRY D'HOLBACH (Baron D'Holbach)
1723–1789

Theology

Theology is but the ignorance of natural causes reduced to a system. . . . [It] is a science that has for its object only things incomprehensible. Contrary to all other sciences, it treats only of what cannot fall under our senses. Hobbes calls it the kingdom of darkness. It is a country in which everything is governed by laws contrary to those which men can recognize in the world they inhabit. In this marvellous region, light is no more than darkness; evidence is doubtful or false; impossibilities are credible; reason is a deceitful guide; and good sense becomes madness. This science is called theology, and this theology is a continual insult to the reason of man. . . .

Does it require anything but plain common sense to perceive that a being incompatible with the obvious facts of experience; that a cause continually opposed to the effects which we attribute to it; that a being of whom we can say nothing without falling into contradiction: that a being who, far from explaining the mysteries of the universe, only makes them more inexplicable: that a being to whom for so many centuries men have so vainly addressed themselves to obtain their happiness and the end of their sufferings: does it, I say, require anything more than plain common sense to perceive that the idea of such a being is an idea without object? . . . Does it, at least, require more than common sense to realize that it is folly and madness for men to hate and torment one another about unintelligible opinions concerning a being of this kind? In short, does not everything prove that morality and virtue are totally incompatible with the notions of a God, whom his ministers and interpreters have described, in every country, as the most capricious, unjust and cruel of tyrants, whose pretended will, however, must serve as law and rule to the inhabitants of the earth?

Good Sense (1772), Preface and Chap. II, trans. H.D. Robinson

Divine Justice

Theologians repeatedly tell us that God is infinitely just, but that his justice is not the justice of man. Of what kind or nature then is this divine justice? What idea can I form of a justice, which so often resembles injustice? Is it not to confound all ideas of just and unjust, to say that what is equitable in God is iniquitous in his creatures? How can we receive for our model a being, whose divine virtues are precisely the opposite of human virtues?

Ibid., Chap. LXXXIX

Universal Consent

Theologians try to silence those who deny the existence of a God, by saying that all men, in all ages and countries, have acknowledged the government of some divinity or other; that every people upon earth have believed in an invisible and powerful being, who has been the object of their worship and veneration; in short that there is no nation, however primitive, that is not convinced of the existence of some intelligence superior to the human. But can an error be changed into truth by the belief of all men? A great philosopher[1] has justly said that 'general tradition, or the universal consent of mankind, is no criterion of truth'; and another wise man before him[2] said that 'a host of learned doctors would not suffice to alter the nature of error, and to transform it into truth.'

There was a time when all men believed that the sun moved round the earth, while the earth remained stationary at the centre of the whole system of the universe. Little more than two centuries have elapsed since this belief was proved false. There was a time, when people would not believe in the existence of the Antipodes, and when those who had the temerity to assert it, were persecuted. Now, no informed man dares to doubt it. All over the world, the masses still believe in sorcerers, ghosts, apparitions and spirits, but no man of sense feels obliged to accept these absurdities. But the most sensible men feel it their duty to believe in a universal spirit!

Ibid., Chap. CXIX

1. Bayle.
2. Averroës.

Atheism and Morality

It is asked, what motives an atheist can have to do good. The motive to please himself and his fellow-creatures; to live happily and peaceably; to gain the affection and esteem of men, whose existence is much more certain, and whose dispositions are much better known, than those of a being by nature unknowable. 'Can he who fears not the gods, fear anything?' He can fear men; he can fear contempt, dishonour, the punishment of the laws; and he can fear himself, and the remorse felt by all those who are conscious of having incurred or merited the hatred of their fellow-creatures. . . .

It is asserted that the dogma of another life is of the utmost importance to the peace and happiness of societies; that without it, men would have no motive to do good. What need is there of terrors and fables to make every rational man aware of how he ought to conduct himself upon earth? Does not everyone see that he has the greatest interest in earning the approval, esteem and benevolence of those who surround him, and in abstaining from everything by which he may incur the censure, contempt and resentment of society? . . . If life is but a passage, let us strive to make it easy; which we cannot do, if we fail in regard for those who travel with us.

Religion, occupied with its gloomy reveries, considers man merely as a pilgrim upon earth; and supposes that, in order to travel more safely, he must forsake company and renounce the pleasures and amusements that might console him for the tediousness and fatigue of the road. A stoical and morose philosopher sometimes gives us advice as irrational as that of religion. But a more rational philosophy invites us to spread flowers on the road of life, to dispel melancholy and panic terrors, to connect our interest with that of our fellow travellers, and by gaiety and lawful pleasures to divert our attention from the difficulties and hazards to which we are often exposed; it teaches us that, to travel agreeably, we should abstain from what might be injurious to ourselves, and carefully shun what might render us odious to our associates.

Ibid., Chaps. CLXVII, CLXVIII

ADAM SMITH
1723–1790

The Death of Hume

Dear Sir

It is with a real, though a very melancholy pleasure, that I sit down to give you some account of the behaviour of our late excellent friend, Mr. Hume, during his last illness. . . .

Upon his return to Edinburgh, though he found himself much weaker, yet his cheerfulness never abated, and he continued to divert himself, as usual, with correcting his own works for a new edition, with reading books of amusement, with the conversation of his friends; and, sometimes in the evening, with a party at his favourite game of whist. His cheerfulness was so great, and his conversation and amusements run so much in their usual strain, that, notwithstanding all bad symptoms, many people could not believe he was dying. 'I shall tell your friend, Colonel Edmondstone', said Doctor Dundas to him one day, 'that I left you much better, and in a fair way of recovering.' 'Doctor', said he, 'as I believe you would not choose to tell any thing but the truth, you had better tell him, that I am dying as fast as my enemies, if I have any, could wish, and as easily and cheerfully as my best friends could desire. . . .'

(On my last visit) I told him, that though I was sensible how very much he was weakened . . . yet his cheerfulness was still so great, the spirit of life seemed still to be so very strong in him, that I could not help entertaining some faint hopes. He answered, 'Your hopes are groundless. . . . When I lie down in the evening, I feel myself weaker than when I rose in the morning; and when I rise in the morning, weaker than when I lay down in the evening. I am sensible, besides, that some of my vital parts are affected, so that I must soon die.' 'Well', said I, 'if it must be so, you have at least the satisfaction of leaving all your friends, your brother's family in particular, in great prosperity.' He said that he felt that satisfaction so sensibly, that when he was reading a few days before, Lucian's *Dialogues of the Dead*, among all the excuses which are alleged to Charon for not entering readily into his boat, he could not find one that fitted him; he had no house to finish, he had no daughter to provide for, he had no enemies upon whom he wished to revenge himself. 'I could not well imagine', said he, 'what excuse I could make to Charon in order to obtain a little delay. . . .' He then diverted himself with inventing several jocular excuses, which he supposed he might make to Charon, and with imagining the very surly answers which it might suit the character of Charon to return to them. 'Upon further consideration', said he, 'I thought I might say to him, "Good Charon, I have been correcting my works for a new edition. Allow me a little time, that I may see how the Public receives the alterations." But Charon would answer, "When you have seen the effect of these, you will be for making other alterations. There will be no end of such excuses; so, honest friend, please step into the boat." But I might still urge, "Have a little patience, good Charon, I have been endeavouring to open the eyes of the Public. If I live a few years longer, I may have the satisfaction of seeing the downfall of some of the prevailing systems of superstition." But Charon would then lose all temper and decency. "You loitering rogue, that will not happen these many hundred years. Do you fancy I will grant you a lease for so long a term? Get into the boat this instant, you lazy loitering rogue." '

But, though Mr. Hume always talked of his approaching dissolution with great cheerfulness, he never affected to make any parade of his magnanimity. He never mentioned the subject but when the conversation naturally led to it, and never dwelt longer upon it than the course of the conversation happened to require. . . .

(Adam Smith then relates how he learned the news of Hume's death.)

Thus died our most excellent, and never to be forgotten friend; concerning whose philosophical opinions men will, no doubt, judge variously . . . but concerning whose character and conduct there can scarce be a difference of opinion. . . . The extreme gentleness of his nature never weakened either the firm-ness of his mind, or the steadiness of his resolutions. His con-stant pleasantry was the genuine effusion of good nature and good-humour, tempered with delicacy and modesty, and without even the slightest tincture of malignity, so frequently the dis-agreeable source of what is called wit in other men. . . . And that gaiety of temper, so agreeable in society, but which is so often accompanied with frivolous and superficial qualities, was in him certainly attended with the most severe application, the most extensive learning, the greatest depth of thought. . . . Upon the whole, I have always considered him, both in his lifetime and since his death, as approaching as nearly to the idea of a per-fectly wise and virtuous man, as perhaps the nature of human frailty will permit.

Letter to William Strahan, 1776

EDWARD GIBBON
1737–1794

Christians and Pagans

When the promise of eternal happiness was proposed to man-kind, on condition of adopting the faith and of observing the pre-cepts of the gospel, it is no wonder that so advantageous an offer should have been accepted by great numbers of every reli-gion, of every rank, and of every province in the Roman empire. The ancient Christians were animated by a contempt for their pre-sent existence, and by a just confidence of immortality, of which the doubtful and imperfect faith of modern ages cannot give us any adequate notion. In the primitive church, the influence of truth was very powerfully strengthened by an opinion which, how-ever it may deserve respect for its usefulness and antiquity, has not been found agreeable to experience. It was universally believed that the end of the world and the kingdom of Heaven were at hand. The near approach of this wonderful event had been predicted by the apostles; the tradition of it was preserved by their earliest disciples, and those who understood in their lit-eral sense the discourses of Christ himself were obliged to expect the second and glorious coming of the Son of Man in the clouds, before that generation was totally extinguished which had beheld his humble condition upon earth, and which might still be witness of the calamities of the Jews under Vespasian or Hadrian. The revolution of seventeen centuries has instructed us not to press too closely the mysterious language of prophecy and revelation; but as long as, for wise purposes, this error was permitted to subsist in the church, it was productive of the most salutary effects on the faith and practice of Christians, who lived in the awful expectation of that moment when the globe itself, and all the various race of mankind, should tremble at the appearance of their divine judge. . . .

Such is the constitution of civil society that, whilst a few persons are distinguished by riches, by honours, and by knowledge, the body of the people is condemned to obscurity, ignorance, and poverty. The Christian religion, which addressed itself to the whole human race, must consequently collect a far greater number of proselytes from the lower than from the superior ranks of life. This innocent and natural circumstance has been improved into a very odious imputation, which seems to be less strenuously denied by the apologists than it is urged by the adversaries of the faith; that the new sect of Christians was almost entirely composed of the dregs of the populace, of peasants and mechanics, of boys and women, of beggars and slaves, the last of whom might sometimes introduce the missionaries into the rich and noble families to which they belonged. These obscure teachers (such was the charge of malice and infidelity) are as mute in public as they are loquacious and dogmatical in private. Whilst they cautiously avoid the dangerous encounter of philosophers, they mingle with the rude and illiterate crowd, and insinuate themselves into those minds whom their age, their sex, or their education has the best disposed to receive the impression of superstitious terrors.

This unfavourable picture, though not devoid of a faint resemblance, betrays, by its dark colouring and distorted features, the pencil of an enemy. As the humble faith of Christ diffused itself through the world, it was embraced by several persons who derived some consequence from the advantages of nature or fortune. . . . In the reign of Diocletian the palace, the courts of justice, and even the army concealed a multitude of Christians who endeavoured to reconcile the interests of the present with those of a future life.

And yet these exceptions are either too few in number, or too recent in time, entirely to remove the imputation of ignorance and obscurity which has been so arrogantly cast on the first proselytes of Christianity. Instead of employing in our defence the fictions of later ages, it will be more prudent to convert the occasion of scandal into a subject of edification. Our serious thoughts will suggest to us that the apostles themselves were chosen by providence among the fishermen of Galilee, and that, the lower we depress the temporal condition of the first Christians, the more reason we shall find to admire their merit and success. It is incumbent on us diligently to remember that the kingdom of heaven was promised to the poor in spirit, and that minds afflicted by calamity and the contempt of mankind cheerfully listen to the divine promise of future happiness; while, on the contrary, the fortunate are satisfied with the possession of this world; and the wise abuse in doubt and dispute their vain superiority of reason and knowledge.

We stand in need of such reflections to comfort us for the loss of some illustrious characters, which in our eyes might have seemed the most worthy of the heavenly present. The names of Seneca, of the elder and the younger Pliny, of Tacitus, of Plutarch, of Galen, of the slave Epictetus, and of the emperor Marcus Antoninus, adorn the age in which they flourished, and exalt the dignity of human nature. They filled with glory their respective stations, either in active or contemplative life; their excellent understandings were improved by study; philosophy had purified their minds from the prejudices of the popular superstition; and their days were spent in the pursuit of truth and the practice of virtue. Yet all these sages (it is no less an object of surprise than of concern) overlooked or rejected the perfection of the Christian system. Their language or their silence equally discover their contempt for the growing sect, which in their time had diffused itself over the Roman Empire. Those among them who condescend to mention the Christians consider them only as obstinate and perverse enthusiasts, who exacted an implicit submission to their mysterious doctrines, without being able to produce a single argument that could engage the attention of men of sense and learning. . . .

But how shall we excuse the supine inattention of the pagan and philosophic world to those evidences which were presented bv the hand of Omnipotence, not to their reason, but to their senses? During the age of Christ, of his apostles, and of their first disciples, the doctrine which they preached was confirmed by innumerable prodigies. The lame walked, the blind saw, the sick were healed, the dead were raised, daemons were expelled, and the laws of Nature were frequently suspended for the benefit of the church. But the sages of Greece and Rome turned aside from the awful spectacle, and pursuing the ordinary occupations of life and study appeared unconscious of any alterations in the moral or physical government of the world. Under the reign of Tiberius, the whole earth, or at least a celebrated province of the Roman Empire, was involved in a praeternatural darkness of three hours. Even this miraculous event, which ought to have excited the wonder, the curiosity, and the devotion of mankind, passed without notice in an age of science and history. It happened during the lifetime of Seneca and the elder Pliny, who must have experienced the immediate effects, or received the earliest intelligence, of the prodigy. Each of these philosophers, in a laborious work, has recorded all the great phenomena of Nature, earthquakes, meteors, comets, and eclipses, which his indefatigable curiosity could collect. Both the one and the other have omitted to mention the greatest phenomenon to which the mortal eye has been witness since the creation of the globe. A distinct chapter of Pliny is designed for eclipses of an extraordinary nature and unusual duration; but he contents himself with describing the singular defect of light which followed the murder of Caesar, when during the greatest part of the year, the orb of the sun appeared pale and without splendour. This season of obscurity, which cannot surely be compared with the praeternaturai darkness of the Passion, had been already celebrated by most of the poets and historians of that memorable age.

Decline and Fall of the Roman Empire, **Vol.1 (1776), Chap. XV**

THOMAS PAINE
1737–1809

Revealed Religion and Morality

The most detestable wickedness, the most horrid cruelties, and the greatest miseries that have afflicted the human race, have had their origin in this thing called revelation, or revealed religion. . . . Whence arose the horrid assassinations of whole nations of men, women and infants, with which the Bible is filled; and the bloody persecutions and tortures unto death, and religious wars, that since that time have laid Europe in blood and ashes; whence arose they, but from this impious thing called revealed religion, and this monstrous belief that God has spoken to man? . . .

Some Christians pretend that Christianity was not established by the sword but of what period of time do they speak? It was impossible that twelve men should begin with the sword: they had not the power; but no sooner were the professors of Christianity sufficiently powerful to employ the sword than they did so, and the stake and the faggot too. . . . Besides this, Christianity grounds itself originally upon the Bible (i.e. the Old Testament) and the Bible was established altogether by the sword, and that in the worst use of it, not to terrify, but to extirpate. The Jews made no converts: butchered all. The Bible is the fire of the Testament (i.e. the New Testament), and both are called the word of God. The Christians read both books; the ministers preach from both books; and this thing call Christianity is made up of both. It is then false to say that Christinaity was not established by the sword. The only sect that have not persecuted are the Quakers, and the only reason that can be given for it is that they are rather Deists than Christians. They do not believe much about Jesus Christ, and they call the scriptures a dead letter. Had they called them by a worse name they had been nearer the truth.

It is incumbent on every man who reverences the character of the Creator, and who wishes to lessen the catalogue of artificial miseries and remove the cause that has sown persecutions thick among mankind, to expel all ideas of revealed religion as a dangerous heresy and an impious fraud. What is it that we have learned from this pretended thing called revealed religion? Nothing that is useful to man, and everything that is dishonourable to his maker. . . .

As to the fragments of morality that are irregularly and thinly scattered in those books, they make no part of this pretended thing—revealed religion. They are the natural dictates of conscience, and the bonds with which society is held together, and without which it cannot exist; and are nearly the same in all religions and all societies. The (New) Testament teaches nothing new upon this subject; and where it attempts to exceed it becomes mean and ridiculous. . . .

It is incumbent on man, as a moralist, that he does not revenge an injury; and it is equally as good in a political sense, for there is no end to retaliation; each retaliates on the other, and calls it justice. (But) loving enemies is (a) dogma of feigned morality; . . . to love in proportion to the injury, if it could be done, would be to offer a premium for a crime. Besides, the word enemies is too vague and general to be used in a moral maxim, which ought always to be clear and defined, like a proverb. If a man be the enemy of another from mistake and prejudice, as in the case of religious opinions, and sometimes in politics, that man is different to an enemy at heart with a criminal intention; and it is incumbent upon us, and it contributes also to our own tranquillity, that we put the best construction upon a thing that it will bear. But even this erroneous motive in him makes no motive for love on the other part; and to say that we can love voluntarily, and without a motive is morally and physically impossible.

Morality is injured by prescribing to it duties that, in the first place, are impossible to be performed; and if they could be would be productive of evil; or, as before said, be premiums for crime. The maxim of doing as we would be done unto does not include this strange doctrine of loving enemies, for no man expects to be loved himself for his crime or his enmity.

Those who preach this doctrine of loving their enemies are in general the greatest persecutors, and they act consistently by so doing; for the doctrine is hypocritical, and it is natural that hypocrisy should act the reverse of what it preaches. For my own part, I disown the doctrine, and consider it as a feigned or fabulous morality; yet the man does not exist that can say I have persecuted him or any set of men, either in the American revolution, or in the French revolution. But it is not incumbent on man to reward a bad action with a good one, or to return good for evil; and wherever it is done, it is a voluntary act, and not a duty.

The Age of Reason, **Part II (1796)**

CONDORCET
1743–1794

The Future Progress of the Human Mind

If man can, with almost complete assurance, predict phenomena when he knows their laws, and if, even when he does not, he can still, with great expectation of success, forecast the future on the basis of his experience of the past, why, then, should it be regarded as a fantastic undertaking to sketch, with some pretence to truth, the future destiny of man on the basis of his history? The sole foundation for belief in the natural sciences is this idea, that the general laws directing the phenomena of the universe, known or unknown, are necessary and constant. Why should this principle be any less true for the development of the intellectual and moral faculties of man than for the other operations of nature? Since beliefs founded on past experience of like conditions provide the only rule of conduct for the wisest of men, why should the philosopher be forbidden to base his conjecture on these same foundations, so long as he does not attribute to them certainty superior to that warranted by the number, the constancy, and th accuracy of his observations?

Our hopes for the future conditions of the human race can be subsumed under three important heads: the abolition of inequality between nations, the progress of equality within each nation, and the true perfection of mankind. Will all nations one day attain that state of civilization which the most enlightened, the freeest and the least burdened by prejudices, such as the French and the Anglo-Americans, have attained already? Will the vast gulf that separates these people from the slavery of nations under the rule of monarchs, from the barbarism of African tribes, from the ignorance of savages little by little disappear?

Is there on the face of the earth a nation whose inhabitants have been debarred by nature herself from the enjoyment of freedom and the exercise of reason?

Are those differences which have hitherto been seen in every civilized country in respect of the enlightenment, the resources, and the wealth enjoyed by the different classes into which it is divided, is that inequality between men which was aggravated or perhaps produced by the earliest progress of society, are these part of civilization itself, or are they due to the present imperfections of the social art? Will they necessarily decrease and ultimately make way for a real equality, the final end of the social art, in which even the effects of the natural differences between men will be mitigated and the only kind of inequality to persist will be that which is in the interests of all and which favours the progress of civilization, of education, and of industry, without entailing either poverty, humiliation, or dependence? In other words, will men approach a condition in which everyone will have the knowledge necessary to conduct himself in the ordinary affairs of life according to the light of his own reason, to preserve his mind free from prejudice, to understand his rights and to exercise them in accordance with his conscience and his creed; in which everyone will become able, through the development of his faculties, to find the means of providing for his needs and in which at last misery and folly will be the exception, and no longer the habitual lot of a section of society?

**from *Sketch for a Historical Picture of
the Progress the Human Mind* (1794)**

JEREMY BENTHAM
1748–1832

Ethical Hedonism

Every pleasure is *prima facie* good, and ought to be pursued. Every pain is *prima facie* evil, and ought to be avoided. . . .

Every act whereby pleasure is reaped is, all consequences apart, good.

Every act by which pleasure is reaped, without any result of pain, is pure gain to happiness; every act whose results of pain are less than the results of pleasure, is good, to the extent of the balance in favour of happiness. . . .

To warrant the assumption that any given act is an evil one, it is incumbent on him who impugns it to shew, not only that evil will be the result of it, but that the sum of evil will be greater than the sum of good which it produces. . . .

The value of pains and pleasures must be estimated by their intensity, duration, certainty, proximity, and extent. Their intensity, duration, proximity, and certainty, respect individuals; their extent the number of persons under their influence. The greater amount of any of these qualities may counterbalance the lesser amount of any other. . . .

Into these regions, then, of pain and pleasure, it is the business of the moralist to bring all human actions, in order to decide on their character of propriety or impropriety, vice or virtue. . . .

Morality is the art of maximizing happiness: it gives the code of laws by which that conduct is suggested whose result will, the whole of human existence being taken into account, leave the greatest quantity of felicity. . . .

Virtue is the preference given to a greater good in comparison with a less: but it is called upon for its exercise when the lesser good is magnified by its adjacency, and the greater good diminished by its remoteness. In the self-regarding part of the field of conduct, it is the sacrifice of a present inclination to a distant personal recompense. In the social part, it is the sacrifice of a man's own pleasure for the benefit of others. The sacrifice is either positive or negative—positive when it is the abandonment of pleasure, negative when it is the subjection to pain.

Deontology, or the Science of Morality (1834),
Vol. I, Chaps. IV, X; Vol. II, Chap. I

Ethical Hedonism in Practice

The moral sense, say some, prompts to generosity, but does it determine what is generous? It prompts to justice, but does it determine what is just?

It can decide no controversy—it can reconcile no difference. Introduce a modern partisan of the moral sense, and an ancient Greek, and ask each of them whether actions deemed blameless

in ancient days, but respecting which opinions have now under-
gone great change, ought to be tolerated in a community. By no
means, says the modern; as my moral sense abhors them, ther-
fore they ought not. But mine, says the ancient, approves of
them; therefore they ought. And there, if the modern keep his
principles and his temper, the matter must end between them.
Upon the ground of moral sense there is no going one jot further;
. . . the modern, (however) as probably he will keep neither his
principles nor his temper, says to the ancient, 'Your moral sense
is nothing to the purpose; yours is corrupt, abominable,
detestable: all nations cry out against you.' 'No such thing', replies
the ancient; 'and if they did, it would be nothing to the purpose;
our business was to inquire, not what people think, but what they
ought to think.' Thereupon the modern kicks the ancient, or spits
in his face. . . . One can think of no other method that is at once
natural and consistent, of continuing the debate.

If you can persuade them both to take the principle of utility*
for their guide, the discourse will take another turn; the result will
be either that they will agree, or that if they disagree, it will be
about some facts; and there is no occasion for supposing either
of them to be so unreasonable as to be angry with his opponent
for entertaining a different opinion from his own concerning a
matter of fact; they will separate with a resolution to make
inquiries that tend to clear up some of the facts, if they are in their
nature capable of being cleared up to the satisfaction of the
inquiring party, or in the conviction of the impossibility of coming
to an agreement, with the resolution of each acting up to his own
opinion, satisfied, at least in some degree, with seeing upon what
the point of the dispute turns. . . .

Men there are who think the cause of truth betrayed by
exposing it to doubt, by making it the object of inquiry. Let them
say whether they think an inquiry of this calm and unimpassioned
kind, could possibly end in the justification of murder, robbery,
theft, devastation, malicious mischief, perjury, or any of those
crimes which are generally dreaded as mortal to the peace of
society? If not, then, either the actions in question are not of the

---

*I.e. the principle that the rightness or wrongness of an act depends on its
tendency to increase or diminish happiness. (Ed.)

same malignant nature, in which case there is no reason why they should be treated as if they were, or if they are of the same malignant nature, the inquiry will show them to be so.

Ibid., Vol. I, Chap. IV

Tampering with Veracity

Veracity is one of the most important bases of human society. The due administration of justice absolutely depends upon it; whatever tends to weaken it, saps the foundations of morality, security, and happiness. The more we reflect on its importance, the more we shall be astonished that legislators have so indiscreetly multiplied the operations which tend to weaken its influence. . . .

In the university of Oxford, among whose members the greater number of ecclesiastical benefices are bestowed, and which even for laymen is the most fashionable place of education,—when a young man presents himself for admission, his tutor, who is generally a clergyman, and the vice-chancellor, who Is also a clergyman, put into his hands a book of statutes, of which they cause him to swear to observe every one. At the same time, it is perfectly well-known to this vice-chancellor and to this tutor, that there never has been any person who was able to observe all these statutes. It is thus that the first lesson this young man learns, and the only lesson he is sure to learn, is a lesson of perjury.

Nor is this all: his next step is to subscribe, in testimony of his belief, to a dogmatical formulary composed about two centuries ago, asserted by the Church of England to be infallibly true, and by most other churches believed to be as infallibly false. By this expedient, one class of men is excluded, while three classes are-admitted. The class excluded is composed of men who, either from a sense of honour, or from conscientious motives, cannot prevail upon themselves publicly and deliberately to utter a lie. The classes admitted consist—1. Of those who literally believe these dogmas; 2. Of those who disbelieve them; 3. Of those who sign them as they would sign the Alcoran, without knowing what they sign, or what they think about it. A nearly similar practice is pursued at Cambridge; and from these two sources the clergy of the Church of England are supplied.

Socrates was accused as a corrupter of youth. What was

meant by this accusation, I know not. But this I know, that to instruct the young in falsehood and perjury, is to corrupt them.

The Rationale of Reward (1825), **Book I, Chap. VIII, 5**

WILLIAM GODWIN
1756–1836

Incredible Beliefs

The good sense of the human mind teaches us the preposterousness of the idea, that the great Father of us all, who dispassionately surveys the creatures He has made, should doom any—and much less the greater part of mankind—to live for ever the victims of unmitigated torment. We find our apprehension incommensurate to such a view of things. In the cool review that we take of these doctrines, our mind refuses to admit them as descriptive of realities. The majority of the inhabitants of Christian countries confess them with their mouths, but deny them in their hearts.

But it was otherwise in the dawn of the gospel. When these views of a future state were first declared to mankind; when these denunciations were thundered in the ears of men by Jesus and his apostles; when, as it appeared to the bystanders, the truth of the doctrine was confirmed by many and stupendous miracles, all persons, except such as retained their sobriety in the midst of a contagious delusion, or who contented themselves with deriding what their neighbours considered as most serious, received the doctrine into their inmost hearts. They exclaimed with consternation to Peter and to the rest of the apostles, 'Men and brethren, what shall we do?' (Acts 2.37)

To the proper apostolic age succeeded a period, when literature and the due cultivation of the mind were banished from the world. There was scarcely such a thing as reason and sound logic anywhere to be found. Men were blinded by superstition, and victims of the grossest credulity. The ghosts of the departed perpetually walked the earth; and there was scarcely a man that had not seen them. Omens and prognostications governed the world. Sorcery and the black art were trades that thrived beyond all others. When judgement and good sense were banished from among mankind, the doctrine of eternal torments found good acceptance. The mind of man did not revolt from the idea that our 'almighty and most merciful Father' should inflict them without remorse and mitigation. Whatever men heard from their spiritual instructors, they admitted without examination and scruple. These were the days when the mass of the people, and indeed all without distinction, were prepared, according to the Scripture phrase, to 'swallow a camel.'

**from *Essays by the late William Godwin*
(published posthumously 1873)**

Liberty

In the heart of every man is indelibly imprinted the love of liberty. The more generous his temper, and the more noble his nature, the more securely does this love exist within it; and till the last breath of his life expires he will hug it to his bosom, and not part with it, as long as he has any force in a tendon or a muscle by means of which it may be grasped.

We know in a manner intuitively the condition of our human life. We are members of a community. We are indissolubly connected with the society of our fellowmen. We have duties. We can perform actions that are worthy of applause; and we can commit crimes and offences against others. We easily reconcile ourselves to this inevitable condition of our existence, and believe that, if we neglect our duties, we must expect in some way or other to be made accountable for it.

But we look for limits to our task. We are contented to be restrained; but we are contented for our whole lives to dance in fetters. We expect that there is a time when we may lay down our load, stretch out limbs in the shade, and say, 'Now I am all my own.'

For the greater and more serious actions of our lives we are accountable. We are contented to be amenable to the laws of society for our delinquencies, and to God, if there be a God that knows and concerns himself with our proceedings, for having neglected to make the best use of our faculties, and on the supposition that we have 'hid our talent in a napkin'.

But we claim as our own peculiar province our innocence— innocence, in the strict and etymological sense of the word, that by which by no construction we can do any harm, when already every duty has been discharged, every debt paid to the uttermost penny. It is not much that we claim; but that little is not on that account the less precious to us.

Ibid., Essay X

ARTHUR SCHOPENHAUER
1788–1860

Early Indoctrination

Philalethes. Religions admittedly appeal, not to conviction as the result of argument, but to belief as demanded by revelation. And as the capacity for believing is strongest in childhood, special care is taken to make sure of this tender age. This has much more to do with the doctrines of belief taking root than threats and reports of miracles. If, in early childhood, certain fundamental views and doctrines are paraded with unusual solemnity, and an air of the greatest earnestness never before visible in anything else; if, at the same time, the possibility of a doubt about them be completely passed over, or touched upon only to indicate that doubt is the first step to eternal perdition, the resulting impression will be so deep that, as a rule . . . doubt about them will be almost as impossible as doubt about one's own existence. Hardly one in ten thousand will have the strength of mind to ask himself seriously and earnestly—is that true?

Religion: a Dialogue (1851), trans. T. B. Saunders

Religion and Ignorance

Philalethes. As you know, religions are like glow-worms; they shine only when it is dark. A certain amount of general ignorance is the condition of all religions, the element in which alone they can exist. . . . Perhaps the time is approaching which has so often been prophesied, when religion will take her departure from European humanity, like a nurse which the child has outgrown; the child will now be given over to the instructions of a tutor. For there is no doubt that religious doctrines which are founded merely on authority, miracles and revelations, are only suited to the childhood of humanity.

Ibid.

Paganism and Christianity

Philalethes. The ancient world was unquestionably less cruel than the Middle Age, with its deaths by exquisite torture, its innumerable burnings at the stake. The ancients, further, were very enduring, laid great stress on justice, frequently sacrificed themselves for their country, showed such traces of every kind of magnanimity, and such genuine manliness, that to this day an acquaintance with their thoughts and actions is called the study of Humanity. The fruits of Christianity were religious wars, butcheries, crusades, inquisitions. . . . Those special moral delinquencies for which we reproach the ancients, and which are perhaps less uncommon now-a-days than appears on the surface to be the case, are trifles compared with the Christian enormities I have mentioned. Can you then, all considered, maintain that mankind has been really made morally better by Christianity?

Ibid.

Religious and Legal Sanctions

Philalethes. Just think: if a public proclamation were suddenly made, announcing the repeal of all the criminal laws, I fancy neither you nor I would have the courage to go home from here under the protection of religious motives. If, in the same way, all religions were declared untrue, we could, under the protection of the laws alone, go on living as before, without any special addition to our apprehensions or our measures of precaution.

Ibid.

Pantheism

The chief objection I have to Pantheism is that it says nothing. To call the world 'God' is not to explain it: it is only to enrich our language with a superfluous synonym for the word 'world'.

A Few Words on Pantheism (1851)

PERCY BYSSHE SHELLEY
1792–1822

Christianity in Action

It is sufficiently evident that an omniscient being never conceived the design of reforming the world by Christianity. Omniscience would surely have foreseen the inefficacy of that system, which experience demonstrates not only to have been utterly impotent in restraining, but to have been most active in exhaling the malevolent propensities of men. During the period which elapsed between the removal of the seat of empire to Constantinople in 328, and its capture by the Turks in 1453, what salutary influence did Christianity exercise upon that world which it was intended to enlighten? Never before was Europe the theatre of such ceaseless and sanguinary wars: never were the people so brutalized by ignorance and debased by slavery.

I will admit that one prediction of Jesus Christ has been indisputably fulfilled. *I come not to bring peace upon earth, but a sword.* Christianity indeed has equalled Judaism in the atrocities, and exceeded it in the extent of its desolation. Eleven millions of men, women, and children, have been killed in battle, butchered in their sleep, burned to death at public festivals of sacrifice, poisoned, tortured, assassinated, and pillaged in the spirit of the Religion of Peace, and for the glory of the most merciful God.

In vain will you tell me that these terrible effects flow not from Christianity, but from the abuse of it. No such excuse will avail to palliate the enormities of a religion pretended to be divine. A limited intelligence is only so far responsible for the effects of its agency as it foresaw, or might have foreseen them; but Omniscience is manifestly chargeable with all the consequences of its conduct. Christianity itself declares that the worth of the tree is to be determined by the quality of its fruit. The extermination of infidels: the mutual persecutions of hostile sects; the midnight massacres and slow burning of thousands, because their creed contained either more or less than the orthodox standard, of which Christianity has been the immediate occasion; and the invariable opposition which philosophy has ever encountered from the spirit of revealed religion, plainly show that a very slight portion of sagacity was sufficient to have estimated at its true value the advantages of that belief to which some Theists are unaccountably attached.

A Refutation of Deism (1814)

HEINRICH HEINE
1797–1856

Pictures of Priests

The priests in Italy have long settled down into harmony with public opinion; the people there are so accustomed to distinguish between clerical dignity and priests without dignity, that they can honour the one even when they despise the other. Even the contrast which the ideal duties and requirements of the spiritual condition form with the unconquerable demands of sensuous nature—that infinitely old, eternal conflict between the spirit and matter—makes of the Italian priest a standing character of popular humour in satires, songs and novels. Similar phenomena are to be found all the world over where there is a like priestly rank, as, for instance, in Hindostan. In the comedies of this primevally pious land, as we have remarked in the *Sacuntala*, and find confirmed in the more recently translated *Vasantasena*, a Brahmin always plays the comic part, or, as we might say, the priest-harlequin, without the least disturbance of the reverence due to his sacrificial functions and his privileged holiness—as little, in fact, as an Italian would experience in hearing of mass or confession to a priest whom he had found the day before tipsy in the mud of the street. In Germany it is different; there the Catholic priest will not only set forth his dignity by his office, but also his office by his person; and because he perhaps in the beginning was in earnest with his calling, and subsequently found that his vows of chastity and of poverty conflicted somewhat with the old Adam, he will not publicly violate them (particularly lest by so doing he might lay himself open to our friend Krug of Leipsig), and so endeavours to assume at least the appearance of a holy life. Hence sham holiness, hypocrisy, and the gloss of outside piety among German priests, while with the Italians the mask is more transparent, manifesting also a certain plump, fat irony, and a digestion of the world passing right comfortably.

But what avail such general reflections? They would be of but little use to you, dear reader, if you had a desire to write against the Catholic priesthood. To do this, one should see with his own eyes the faces thereunto pertaining. Of a truth it is not enough to have seen them in the royal opera-house in Berlin. The last head-manager did his best to make the coronation array in the *Maid of Orleans* true to life, to give his fellow-countrymen an accurate idea of a procession, and to show them priests of every colour. But the most accurate costumes cannot supply the original coun-tenances, and though an extra hundred thousand dollars should be fooled away for gold mitres, festooned surplices, embroidered chasubles, and similar stuff, still the cold reasoning Protestant noses which come protesting out from beneath the mitres afore-said, the lean meditative legs which peep from under the white lace of the surplices, and the enlightened bellies, a world too wide for the chasubles, would all remind one of us that it was not Catholic clergymen, but Berlin worldlings which wander over the stage.

from *Pictures of Travel. City of Lucca* (1828)

AUGUSTE MARIE FRANÇOIS XAVIER COMTE
1798–1857

Positive Ethics

The positive philosophy is the first that has ascertained the true point of view of social morality. The metaphysical philosophy sanctioned egotism; and the theological subordinated real life to an imaginary one; while the new philosophy takes social moral-ity for the basis of its whole system. The two former systems were so little favourable to the rise of the purely disinterested affections, that they often led to a dogmatic denial of their exis-tence. . . . We have yet to witness the moral superiority of a phi-losophy which connects each of us with the whole of human exis-tence, in all times and places. The restriction of our expectations to actual life must furnish new means of connecting our individual development with the universal progression, the growing regard to which will afford the only possible, and the utmost possible, satisfaction to our natural aspiration after eternity. For instance, the scrupulous respect for human life, which has always increased with our social progression, must strengthen more and more as the chimerical hope dies out which disparages the present life as merely accessory to the one in prospect. . . . By its various aptitudes, positive morality will tend more and more to exhibit the happiness of the individual as depending on the complete expansion of benevolent acts and sympathetic emotions towards the whole of our race; and even beyond our race, by a gradual extension to all sentient beings below us, in proportion to their animal rank and their social utility. The relative nature of the new philosophy will render it applicable, with equal facility and accuracy, to the exigencies of each case, individual or social, whereas we see how the absolute character of religious morality has deprived it of almost all force in cases which, arising after its institution, could not have been duly provided for. Till the full rational establishment of positive morality has taken place, it is the business of true philosophers, ever the precursors of their race, to confirm it in the estimation of the world by the sustained superiority of their own conduct, personal, domestic, and social.

The Positive Philosophy, **Introduction (1830)**
Chap I, trans. H. Martineau

LUDWIG FEUERBACH
1804–1872

The Essence of Religion Considered Generally

What we have hitherto been maintaining generally, even with regard to sensational impressions, of the relation between subject and object, applies especially to the relation between the subject and the religious object.

In the perceptions of the senses consciousness of the object is distinguishable from consciousness of self; but in religion, consciousness of the object and self-consciousness coincide. The object of the senses is out of man, the religious object is within him, and therefore as little forsakes him as his self-consciousness or his conscience; it is the intimate, the closest object. 'God', says Augustine, for example, 'is nearer, more related to us, and therefore more easily known by us, than sensible, corporeal things.'* The object of the senses is in itself indifferent—independent of the disposition or of the judgement; but the object of religion is a selected object; the most excellent, the first, the supreme being; it essentially presupposes a critical judgement, a discrimination between the divine and the non-divine, between that which is worthy of adoration and that which is not worthy.† And here may be applied, without any limitation, the proposition: the object of any subject is nothing else than the subject's own nature taken objectively. Such as are a man's thoughts and dispositions, such is his God; so much worth as a man has, so much and no more has his God. Consciousness of God is self-consciousness, knowledge of God is self-knowledge. By his God thou knowest the man, and by the man his God; the two are identical. Whatever is God to a man, that is his heart and soul; and conversely, God is the manifested inward nature, the expressed self of a man,—religion the solemn unveiling of a man's hidden treasures, the revelation of his intimate thoughts, the open confession of his love-secrets.

But when religion—consciousness of God—is designated as the self-consciousness of man, this is not to be understood as affirming that the religious man is directly aware of this identity; for, on the contrary, ignorance of it is fundamental to the peculiar nature of religion. To preclude this misconception, it is better to say, religion is man's earliest and also indirect form of self-knowledge. Hence, religion everywhere precedes philosophy, as in the history of the race, so also in that of the individual. Man first of all sees his nature as if out of himself, before he finds it in himself. His own nature is in the first instance contemplated by him as that of another being. Religion is the childlike condition of humanity; but the child sees his nature—man—out of himself; in childhood

---

*De Genesi ad litteram, lv.c. 16.
†Unusquisque vestrum non cogitat, prius se debere Deum nosse, quam colere.—M. Minucii Felicis Octavianus, c.24.

a man is an object to himself, under the form of another man. Hence the historical progress of religion consists in this: that what by an earlier religion was regarded as objective, is now recognised as subjective; that is, what was formerly contemplated and worshipped as God is now perceived to be something human. What was at first religion becomes at a later period idolatry; man is seen to have adored his own nature. Man has given objectivity to himself, but has not recognised the object as his own nature: a later religion takes this forward step; every advance in religion is therefore a deeper self-knowledge. But every particular religion, while it pronounces its predecessors idolatrous, excepts itself—and necessarily so, otherwise it would no longer be religion—from the fate, the common nature of all religions: it imputes only to other religions what is the fault, if fault it be, of religion in general. Because it has a different object, a different tenour, because it has transcended the ideas of preceding religions, it erroneously supposes itself exalted above the necessary eternal laws which constitute the essence of religion—it fancies its object, its ideas, to be superhuman. But the essence of religion, thus hidden from the religious, is evident to the thinker, by whom religion is viewed objectively, which it cannot be by its votaries. And it is our task to show that the antithesis of divine and human is altogether illusory, that it is nothing else than the antithesis between the human nature in general, and the human individual: that, consequently, the object and contents of the Christian religion are altogether human.

from *The Essence of Christianity* trans. George Eliot (1854)

JOHN STUART MILL
1806–1873

The Utility of Religion

So long as men accepted the teachings of their religion as positive facts, no more a matter of doubt than their own existence or the existence of the objects around them, to ask the use of believing it could not possibly occur to them. The utility of religion did not need to be asserted until the arguments for its truth had in a great measure ceased to convince. People must either have ceased to believe, or have ceased to rely on the belief of others, before they could take that inferior ground of defence without a consciousness of lowering what they were endeavouring to raise. An argument for the utility of religion is an appeal to unbelievers, to induce them to practise a well-meant hypocrisy, or to semi-believers to make them avert their eyes from what might possibly shake their unstable belief, or finally to persons in general to abstain from expressing any doubts they may feel, since a fabric of immense importance to mankind is so insecure at its foundations, that men must hold their breath in its neighbourhood for fear of blowing it down.

In the present period of history, however, we seem to have arrived at a time when, among the arguments for and against religion, those which relate to its usefulness assume an important place. We are in an age of weak beliefs, and in which such belief as men have is much more determined by their wish to believe than by any mental appreciation of evidence. The wish to believe does not arise only from selfish but often from the most disinterested feelings; and though it cannot produce the unwavering and perfect reliance which once existed, . . . it induces people to continue laying out their lives according to doctrines which have lost part of their hold on the mind, and to maintain towards the world the same, or a rather more demonstrative attitude of belief, than they thought it necessary to exhibit when their personal conviction was more complete.

If religious belief be indeed so necessary to mankind, as we are continually assured that it is, there is great reason to lament, that the intellectual grounds of it should require to be backed by moral bribery or subornation of the understanding. . . . It is a most painful position to be drawn in contrary directions by the two noblest of all objects of pursuit, truth, and the general good. . . .

Many, having observed in others or experienced in themselves elevated feelings which they imagine incapable of emanating from any other source than religion, have an honest aversion to anything tending, as they think, to dry up the fountain of such feelings. They, therefore, either dislike and disparage all philosophy, or addict themselves with intolerant zeal to those forms of it in which intuition usurps the place of evidence, and internal feeling is made the test of objective truth. The whole of the prevalent metaphysics of the present century is one tissue of suborned evidence in favour of religion. . . . It is time to consider whether all this straining to prop up beliefs which require so great an expense of intellectual toil and ingenuity to keep them standing, yields any sufficient return in human well-being. . . .

To speak first, then, of religious belief as an instrument of social good. We must commence by drawing a distinction most commonly overlooked. It is usual to credit religion as such with the whole of the power inherent in any system of moral duties inculcated by education and enforced by opinion. Undoubtedly mankind would be in a deplorable state if no principles or precepts of justice, veracity, beneficence, were taught publicly or privately, and if these virtues were not encouraged, and the opposite vices repressed, by the praise and blame, the favourable and unfavourable sentiments of mankind. And since nearly everything of this sort which does take place, takes place in the name of religion; since almost all who are taught any morality whatever, have it taught to them as religion . . . the effect which the teaching produces as teaching, it is supposed to produce as religious teaching, and religion receives the credit of all the influence in human affairs which belongs to any generally accepted system of rules for the guidance and government of human life.

Few persons have sufficiently considered how great an influence this is; what vast efficacy belongs naturally to any doctrine received with tolerable unanimity as true, and impressed on the mind from the earliest childhood as duty. A little reflection will, I think, lead us to the conclusion that it is this which is the great moral power in human affairs, and that religion only seems so powerful because this mighty power has been under its command. . . .

The power of education is almost boundless: there is not one natural inclination which it is not strong enough to coerce, and, if needful, to destroy by disuse. In the greatest recorded victory which education has ever achieved over a whole host of natural inclinations in an entire people—the maintenance through centuries of the institutions of Lycurgus,—it was very little, if even at all, indebted to religion: for the gods of the Spartans were the same as those of other Greek states. . . . It was not religion which formed the strength of the Spartan institutions: the root of the system was devotion to Sparta, to the ideal of the country or State: which transformed into ideal devotion to a greater country, the world, would be equal to that and far nobler achievements. Among the Greeks generally, social morality was extremely independent of religion. . . . The gods were not supposed to concern themselves much with men's conduct to one another, except when men had contrived to make the gods themselves an interested party, by placing an assertion or an engagement under the sanction of a solemn appeal to them, by oath or vow. . . . For the enforcement of human moralities secular inducements were almost exclusively relied on. The case of Greece is, I believe, the only one in which any teaching, other than religious, has had the unspeakable advantage of forming the basis of education: and though much may be said against the quality of some part of the teaching, very little can be said against its effectiveness. The most memorable example of the power of education over conduct, is afforded (as I have just remarked) by this exceptional case; constituting a strong presumption that in other cases, early religious teaching has owed its power over mankind rather to its being early than to its being religious.

'The Utility of Religion', from *Three Essays on Religion* (1874)

Omnipotence and Evil

However offensive the proposition may appear to many religious persons, they should be willing to look in the face the undeniable fact, that the order of Nature, in so far as unmodified by man, is such as no being, whose attributes are justice and benevolence, would have made, with the intention that his rational creatures should follow it as an example. . . .

In sober truth, nearly all the things which men are hanged or imprisoned for doing to one another, are Nature's every day performances. Killing, the most criminal act recognized by human laws, Nature does once to every being that lives; and in a large proportion of cases, after protracted tortures such as only the greatest monsters whom we read of ever purposely inflected on their living fellow-creatures. . . . She mows down those on whose existence hangs the well-being of a whole people, perhaps the prospects of the human race for generations to come, with as little compunction as those whose death is a relief to themselves, or a blessing to those under their noxious influence. Such are Nature's dealings with life. Even when she does not intend to kill, she inflicts the same tortures in apparent wantonness. In the clumsy provision which she has made for that perpetual renewal of animal life, rendered necessary by the prompt termination she puts to it in every individual instance, no human being ever comes into the world but another human being is literally stretched on the rack for hours or days, not unfrequently issuing in death. Next to taking life (equal to it according to a high authority) is taking the means by which we live; and Nature does this too on the largest scale and with the most callous indifference. A single hurricane destroys the hopes of a season; a flight of locusts, or an inundation, desolates a district; a trifling chemical change in an edible root, starves a million of people. . . . Everything, in short, which the worst men commit either against life or property is perpetrated on a larger scale by natural agents. Nature has Noyades more fatal than those of Carrier; her explosions of fire damp are as destructive as human artillery; her plague and cholera far surpass the poison cups of the Borgias. Even the love of 'order' which is thought to be a following of the ways of Nature, is in fact a contradiction of them. All which people are accustomed to deprecate as 'disorder' and its consequences, is precisely a counterpart of Nature's ways. Anarchy and the Reign of Terror are overmatched in injustice, ruin, and death, by a hurricane and a pestilence. . . .

Not even the most distorted and contracted theory of good which ever was framed by religious or philosophical fanaticism, can the government of Nature be made to resemble the work of a being at once good and omnipotent. . . . One only form of belief in the supernatural . . . stands wholly clear both of intellectual contradiction and of moral obliquity. It is that which, resigning irrevocably the idea of an omnipotent creator, regards Nature and Life not as the expression throughout of the moral character and purposes of the Deity, but as the product of a struggle between contriving goodness and an intractable material, as was believed by Plato, or a principle of evil, as was the doctrine of the Manicheans. . . . A virtuous human being assumes in this theory the exalted character of a fellow-labourer with the Highest, a fellow-combatant in the great strife. . . . Against the moral tendency of this creed no possible objection can lie: it can produce on whoever can succeed in believing it, no other than an ennobling effect. The evidence for it, indeed, if evidence it can be called, is too shadowy and unsubstantial, and the promises it holds out too distant and uncertain, to admit of its being a permanent substitute for the religion of humanity; but the two may be held in conjunction: and he to whom ideal good, and the progress of the world towards it, are already a religion, even though that other creed may seem to him a belief not grounded on evidence, is at liberty to indulge the pleasing and encouraging thought that its truth is possible.

'Nature' and 'The Utility of Religion',
from *Three Essays on Religion* (1874)

CHARLES DARWIN
1809–1882

The Social Instincts

Every one will admit that man is a social being. We see this in his dislike of solitude, and in his wish for society beyond that of his own family. Solitary confinement is one of the severest punishments which can be inflicted. Some authors suppose that man primevally lived in single families; but at the present day, though single families, or only two or three together, roam the solitudes of some savage lands, they always, as far as I can discover, hold friendly relations with other families inhabiting the same district. Such families occasionally meet in council, and unite for their common defence. It is no argument against savage man being a social animal, that the tribes inhabiting adjacent districts are almost always at war with each other; for the social instincts never extend to all the individuals of the same species. . . .

The social instincts, which no doubt were acquired by man as by the lower animals for the good of the community, will from the first have given to him some wish to aid his fellows, some feeling of sympathy, and have compelled him to regard their approbation and disapprobation. Such impulses will have served him at a very early period as a rude rule of right and wrong. But as man gradually advanced in intellectual power, and was enabled to trace the more remote consequences of his actions; as he acquired sufficient knowledge to reject baneful customs and superstitions; as he regarded more and more, not only the welfare, but the happiness of his fellow-men; as from habit, following on beneficial experience, instruction and example, his sympathies became more tender and widely diffused, extending to men of all races, to the imbecile, maimed, and other useless members of society, and finally to the lower animals,—so would the standard of his morality rise higher and higher. . . .

As a struggle may sometimes be seen going on between the various instincts of the lower animals, it is not surprising that there should be a struggle in man between his social instincts, with their derived virtues, and his lower, though momentarily stronger impulses or desires. This, as Mr. Galton has remarked, is all the less surprising, as man has emerged from a state of barbarism within a comparatively recent period. After having yielded to some temptation we feel a sense of dissatisfaction, shame, repentance, or remorse, analogous to the feelings caused by other powerful instincts or desires, when left unsatisfied or baulked. We compare the weakened impression of a past temptation with the ever present social instincts, or with habits, gained in early youth and strengthened during our whole lives, until they have become almost as strong as instincts. If with the temptation still before us we do not yield, it is because either the social instincts or some custom is at the moment predominant, or because we have learnt that it will appear to us hereafter the stronger, when compared with the weakened impression of the temptation, and we realize that its violation would cause us suffering. Looking to future generations, there is no cause to fear that the social instincts will grow weaker. . . .

The social instincts,—the prime principle of man's moral constitution—with the aid of active intellectual powers and the effects of habit, naturally lead to the golden rule, 'As ye would that men should do to you, do ye to them likewise'; and this lies at the foundation of morality.

The Descent of Man (1871), Part I, Chap. IV

The Growth of Scepticism

During these two years (1837–1839) I was led to think much about religion. Whilst on board the *Beagle* (1832–1836) I was quite orthodox. . . . But (later) I had gradually come to see that the Old Testament from its manifestly false history of the world, with the Tower of Babel, the rainbow as a sign, etc., etc., and from its attributing to God the feelings of a revengeful tyrant, was no more to be trusted than the sacred books of the Hindoos, or the beliefs of any barbarian. . . .

By further reflecting that the clearest evidence would be requisite to make any sane man believe in the miracles by which Christianity is supported,—that the more we know of the fixed laws of nature the more incredible do miracles become,—that the men at that time were ignorant and credulous to a degree almost incomprehensible by us,—that the Gospels cannot be proved to have been written simultaneously with the events,—that they differ in many important details, far too important as it seemed to me to be admitted as the usual inaccuracies of eyewitnesses;—by such reflections as these, which I give not as having the least novelty or value, but as they influenced me, I gradually came to disbelieve in Christianity as a divine revelation. . . .

Thus disbelief crept over me at a very slow rate, but was at last complete. The rate was so slow that I felt no distress, and have never since doubted even for a single second that my conclusion was correct. I can indeed hardly see how anyone ought to wish Christianity to be true; for if so the plain language of the text seems to show that the men who do not believe, and this would include my father, brother and almost all my best friends, will be everlastingly punished.

And this is a damnable doctrine.

Although I did not think much about the existence of a personal God until a considerably later period of my life, I will here give the vague conclusions to which I have been driven. The old argument of design in nature, as given by Paley, which formerly seemed to me so conclusive, fails, now that the law of natural selection has been discovered. We can no longer argue that, for instance, the beautiful hinge of a bivalve shell must have been made by an intelligent being, like the hinge of a door by man.

There seems to be no more design in the variability of organic beings and in the action of natural selection, than in the course which the wind blows. Everything in nature is the result of fixed laws. . . .

At the present day the most usual argument for the existence of an intelligent God is drawn from the deep inward conviction and feelings which are experienced by most persons. But it cannot be doubted that Hindoos, Mahomadans and others might argue in the same manner and with equal force in favour of the existence of one God, or of many Gods, or as with the Buddhists of no God. There are also many barbarian tribes who cannot be said with any truth to believe in what we call God: they believe indeed in spirits or ghosts, and it can be explained, as Tyler and Herbert Spencer have shown, how such a belief would be likely to arise.

Formerly I was led by feelings such as those just referred to, (although I do not think that the religious sentiment was ever strongly developed in me), to the firm conviction of the existence of God, and of the immortality of the soul. In my Journal I wrote that whilst standing in the midst of the grandeur of a Brazilian forest, 'it is not possible to give an adequate idea of the higher feelings of wonder, admiration, and devotion which fill and elevate the mind.' I well remember my conviction that there is more in man than the mere breath of his body. But now the grandest scenes would not cause any such convictions and feelings to rise in my mind. It may be truly said that I am like a man who has become colour-blind and the universal belief by men of the existence of redness makes my present loss of perception of not the least value as evidence. This argument would be a valid one if all men of all races had the same inward conviction of the existence of one God; but we know that this is very far from being the case. Therefore I cannot see that such inward convictions and feelings are of any weight as evidence of what really exists. The state of mind which grand scenes formerly excited in me, and which was intimately connected with a belief in God, did not essentially differ from that which is often called the sense of sublimity; and however difficult it may be to explain the genesis of this sense, it can hardly be advanced as an argument for the existence of God, any more than the powerful though vague and similar feelings excited by music. . . .

Another source of conviction in the existence of God, connected with the reason and not with the feelings, impresses me as having much more weight. This follows from the extreme difficulty or rather impossibility of conceiving this immense and wonderful universe, including man with his capacity of looking far backwards and far into futurity, as the result of blind chance or necessity. When thus reflecting I feel compelled to look to a First Cause having an intelligent mind in some degree analogous to that of man; and I deserve to be called a Theist.

This conclusion was strong in my mind about the time, as far as I can remember, when I wrote the *Origin of Species:* and it is since that time that it has very gradually with many fluctuations become weaker. But then arises the doubt—can the mind of man, which has, as I fully believe, been developed from a mind as low as that possessed by the lowest animal, be trusted when it draws such grand conclusions; may not these be the result of the connection between cause and effect which strikes us as a necessary one, but probably depends merely on inherited experience? Nor must we overlook the probability of the constant inculcation in a belief in God on the minds of children producing so strong and perhaps an inherited effect on their brains not yet fully developed, that it would be as difficult for them to throw off their belief in God, as for a monkey to throw off its instinctive fear and hatred of a snake.

Autobiography (1958 edition)

MARIAN EVANS ('GEORGE ELIOT')
1819–1880

Pulpit Oratory

(The preacher) has an immense advantage over all other public speakers. The platform orator is subject to the criticism of hisses and groans. Counsel for the plaintiff expects the retort of counsel for the defendant. The honourable gentleman on one side of the House is liable to have his facts and figures shown up by his honourable friend on the opposite side. Even the scientific or literary lecturer, if he is dull or incompetent, may see the best part of his audience slip quietly out one by one. But the preacher is com-

pletely master of the situation: no-one may hiss, no-one may depart. Like the writer of imaginary conversations, he may put what imbecilities he pleases into the mouths of his antagonists, and swell with triumph when he has refuted them. He may riot in gratuitous assertions, confident that no man will contradict him; he may exercise perfect free-will in logic, and invent illustrative experience; he may give an evangelical edition of history with the inconvenient facts omitted;—all this he may do with impunity, certain that those . . . who are not sympathizing are not listening. . . . The clergy are, practically, the most irresponsible of all talkers.
'Evangelical Teaching: Dr. Cumming' (Westminster Review, 1853, reprinted in *Essays and Leaves from a Note-Book,* 1884)

Judicious Haziness

For the most part, the general reader of the present day does not exactly know what distance he goes; he only knows that he does not go 'too far'. Of any remarkable thinker whose writings have excited controversy, he likes to have it said that 'his errors are to be deplored', leaving it not too certain what those errors are: he is fond of what may be called disembodied opinions, that float in vapoury phrases above all systems of thought or action; he likes an undefined Christianity which opposes itself to nothing in particular, an undefined education of the people, an undefined amelioration of all things: in fact, he likes sound views,—nothing extreme, but something between the excesses of the past and the excesses of the present. This modern type of the general reader may be known in conversation by the cordiality with which he assents to indistinct, blurred statements: say that black is black, he will shake his head and hardly think it; say that black is not so very black, he will reply, 'Exactly'. He has no hesitation, if you wish it, even to get up at a public meeting and express his conviction that at times, and within certain limits, the radii of a circle have a tendency to be equal; but, on the other hand, he would urge that the spirit of geometry may be carried a little too far. His only bigotry is a bigotry against any clearly defined opinion; not in the least based on a scientific scepticism, but belonging to a lack of coherent thought,—a spongy texture of mind, that gravitates strongly to nothing. The one thing he is staunch for is the utmost liberty of private haziness.

'The Influence of Rationalism: Lecky's History'
(*Fortnightly Review,* 1865, reprinted in
Essays and Leaves from a Note-Book, 1884)

Truth-telling

So I am content to tell my simple story, without trying to make things seem better than they were; dreading nothing, indeed, but falsity, which, in spite of one's best efforts, there is reason to dread. Falsehood is so easy, truth so difficult. The pencil is conscious of a delightful facility in drawing a griffin—the longer the claws, and the larger the wings, the better; but that marvellous facility which we mistook for genius is apt to forsake us when we want to draw a real unexaggerated lion. Examine your words well, and you will find that even when you have no motive to be false, it is a very hard thing to say the exact truth, even about your own immediate feelings—much harder than to say something fine about them which is not the exact truth.

It is for this rare, precious quality of truthfulness that I delight in many Dutch paintings, which lofty-minded people despise. I find a source of delicious sympathy in these faithful pictures of a monotonous homely existence, which has been the fate of so many more among my fellow-mortals than a life of pomp or of absolute indigence, of tragic suffering or of world-stirring actions. I turn, without shrinking, from cloud-borne angels, from prophets, sibyls, and heroic warriors, to an old woman bending over her flower-pot, or eating her solitary dinner, while the noonday light, softened perhaps by a screen of leaves, falls on her mob-cap, and just touches the rim of her spinning-wheel, and her stone jug, and all those cheap common things which are the precious necessaries of life to her;—or I turn to that village wedding, kept between four brown walls, where an awkward bridegroom opens the dance with a high-shouldered, broad-faced bride, while elderly and middle-aged friends look on, with very irregular noses and lips, and probably with quart-pots in their hands, but with an expression of unmistakable contentment and goodwill.

from *Adam Bede* (1859)

HERBERT SPENCER
1830-1903

Alienation from Christianity

Memory does not tell me the extent of my divergence (at the age of twenty) from current beliefs. There had not taken place any pronounced rejection of them, but they were slowly losing their hold. Their hold had, indeed, never been very decided: 'the creed of Christendom' being evidently alien to my nature, both emotional and intellectual. To many, and apparently to most, religious worship yields a species of pleasure. To me it never did so; unless, indeed, I count as such the emotion produced by sacred music. . . . But the expressions of adoration of a personal being, the utterance of laudations, and the humble professions of obedience, never found in me any echoes. Hence, when left to myself, as at Worcester and previously in London, I spent my Sundays either in reading or in country walks.

In those days there was not any decided conviction about the propriety or impropriety of this course. Criticism had not yet shown me how astonishing is the supposition that the Cause from which have arisen thirty millions of Suns with their attendant planets, took the form of a man, and made a bargain with Abraham to give him territory in return for allegiance. I had not at that time repudiated the notion of a deity who is pleased with the singing of his praises, and angry with the infinitesimal beings he has made when they fail to tell him perpetually of his greatness. It had not become manifest to me how absolutely and immeasurably unjust it would be that for Adam's disobedience (which might have caused a harsh man to discharge his servant), all Adam's guiltless descendants should be damned, with the exception of a relatively few who accepted the 'plan of salvation' which the immense majority had never heard of. Nor had I in those days perceived the astounding nature of the creed which offers for profoundest worship, a being who calmly looks on while myriads of his creatures are suffering eternal torments. But, though no definite propositions of this kind had arisen in me, it is probable that the dim consciousness out of which they eventually emerged, produced alienation from the established beliefs and observances.

Autobiography (1904), Part III, Chap. X

JOSEPH ERNEST RENAN
1823–1892

The Historical Jesus

That Jesus never dreamt of making himself pass for an incarnation of God, is a matter about which there can be no doubt. Such an idea was entirely foreign to the Jewish mind; and there is no trace of it in the synoptical gospels;[1] we only find it indicated in portions of the Gospel of John, which cannot be accepted as expressing the thoughts of Jesus. Sometimes Jesus even seems to take precautions to put down such a doctrine.[2] The accusation that he made himself God, or the equal of God, is presented, even in the Gospel of John, as a calumny of the Jews.[3] In this last Gospel he declares himself less than his Father.[4] Elsewhere he avows that the Father has not revealed everything to him.[5] He believes himself to be more than an ordinary man, but separated from God by an infinite distance. He is Son of God, but all men are, or may become so, in diverse degrees.[6] Every one ought daily to call God his father; all who are raised again will be sons of God.[7] The divine son-ship was attributed in the Old Testament to beings whom it was by no means pretended were equal with God.[8] The word 'son' has the widest meanings in the Semitic language, and in that of the New Testament. . . .

The title 'Son of God', or simply 'Son', thus became for Jesus a title analogous to 'Son of man', and, like that, synonymous with the 'Messiah', with the sole difference that he called himself 'Son of man', and does not seem to have made the same use of the phrase, 'Son of God'.[9]

Jesus appears to have remained a stranger to (the) refinements of theology, which were soon to fill the world with barren disputes. The metaphysical theory of the Word, such as we find it in the writings of his contemporary Philo . . . had nothing in common with Messianism. . . . It was John the Evangelist, or his school, who afterwards endeavoured to prove that Jesus was the Word, and who created, in this sense, quite a new theology, very different from that of the 'kingdom of God'.[10] The essential character of the Word was that of Creator and of Providence. Now, Jesus never pretended to have created the world, nor to govern it. His office was to judge it, to renovate it. The position of president at the final judgment of humanity, was the essential attribute which Jesus attached to himself, and the character which all the first Christians attributed to him.[11] Until the great day, he will sit at the right hand of God, as his Metathronos, his first minister, and his future avenger. The superhuman Christ of the Byzantine apsides, seated as judge of the world, in the midst of the apostles in the same rank with him, and superior to the angels who only assist and serve, is the exact representation of that conception of the 'Son of man', of which we find the first features so strongly indicated in the book of Daniel.

At all events, the strictness of a studied theology by no means existed in such a state of society. . . . We must not look here for either logic or sequence. The need Jesus had of obtaining credence, and the enthusiasm of his disciples, heaped up contradictory notions. To the Messianic believers of the millenarian school, and to the enthusiastic readers of the books of Daniel and of Enoch, he was the Son of man—to the Jews holding the ordinary faith, and to the readers of Isaiah and Micah, he was the Son of David—to the disciples he was the Son of God, or simply the Son. Others, without being blamed by the disciples, took him for John the Baptist risen from the dead, for Elias, for Jeremiah, conformable to the popular belief that the ancient prophets were about to reappear, in order to prepare the time of the Messiah.

The Life of Jesus (1863), Chap. XV, trans. anon.

1. Certain passages, such as Acts 2:22, expressly exclude this idea.
2. Matt, 19:17; Mark 10:18; Luke 18:19.
3. John 5:18ff.; John 10:33ff.
4. John 14:28.
5. Mark 13:32.
6. Matt. 5:9, 45; Luke 3:38, 6:35, 20:36; John 1:12, 13, 10:34, 35.
7. Luke 20:36.
8. Gen. 6:2; 2 Sam. 7:14; Job 1:6, 2:1, 38:7; Ps. 82:6.
9. It is only in the Gospel of John that Jesus uses the expression 'Son of God' or 'Son' in speaking of himself.
10. John 1:1–14; 1 Epistle 5:7; moreover, it will be remarked that in the Gospel of John, the expression of 'the Word' does not occur except in the prologue, and that the narrator never puts it into the mouth of Jesus.
11. Acts 10:42.

THOMAS HENRY HUXLEY
1825–1895

Agnosticism

Agnosticism is not properly described as a 'negative' creed, nor indeed as a creed of any kind, except in so far as it expresses absolute faith in the validity of a principle, which is as much ethical as intellectual. This principle may be stated in various ways, but they all amount to this; that it is wrong for a man to say that he is certain of the objective truth of any proposition unless he can produce evidence which logically justifies that certainty. This is what Agnosticism asserts; and in my opinion, it is all that is essential to Agnosticism. That which Agnostics deny, and repudiate as immoral, is the contrary doctrine, that there are propositions which men ought to believe, without logically satisfactory evidence; and that reprobation ought to attach to the profession of disbelief in such inadequately supported propositions. The justification of the Agnostic principle lies in the success which follows upon its application, whether in the field of natural, or in that of civil, history; and in the fact that, so far as these topics are concerned, no sane man thinks of denying its validity.
    'Agnosticism and Christianity' (*Nineteenth Century,* June 1889, reprinted in *Essays upon Some Controverted Questions,* 1892)

I was brought up in the strictest school of evangelical orthodoxy; and when I was old enough to think for myself I started upon my journey of inquiry with little doubt about the general truth of what I had been taught; and with that feeling of the unpleasantness of being called an 'infidel' which, we are told, is so right and proper. Near my journey's end, I find myself in a condition of something more than mere doubt about these matters.

    In the course of other inquiries, I have had to do with fossil remains which looked quite plain at a distance, and became more and more indistinct as I tried to define their outline by close inspection. There was something there—something which, if I could win assurance about it, might mark a new epoch in the history of the earth; but, study as long as I might, certainty eluded my grasp. So has it been with me in my efforts to define the grand figure of Jesus as it lies in the primary strata of Christian literature. Is he the kindly, peaceful Christ depicted in the Catacombs? Or is he the stern judge who frowns about the altar of SS. Cosmas and Damianus? Or can he be rightly represented by the bleeding ascetic, broken down by physical pain, of too many mediaeval pictures? Are we to accept the Jesus of the second, or the Jesus of the fourth Gospel, as the true Jesus? What did he really say and do; and how much that is attributed to him, in speech and action, is the embroidery of the various parties into which his followers tended to split themselves within twenty years of his death, when even the threefold tradition was only nascent?

If any one will answer these questions for me with something more to the point than feeble talk about the 'cowardice of Agnosticism', I shall be deeply his debtor. Unless and until they are satisfactorily answered, I say of Agnosticism in this matter, '*J'y suis, et j'y reste. . . .*'

I am very well aware, as I suppose most thoughtful people are in these times, that the process of breaking away from old beliefs is extremely unpleasant; and I am much disposed to think that the encouragement, the consolation, and the peace afforded to earnest believers in even the worst forms of Christianity are of great practical advantage to them. What deductions must be made from this gain on the score of the harm done to the citizen by the ascetic other-worldliness of logical Christianity; to the ruler, by the hatred, malice, and all uncharitableness of sectarian bigotry; to the legislator, by the spirit of exclusiveness and domination of those that count themselves pillars of orthodoxy; to the philosopher by the restraints on the freedom of learning and teaching which every Church exercises, when it is strong enough; to the conscientious soul, by the introspective hunting after sins of the mint and cummin type, the fear of theological error, and the overpowering terror of possible damnation, which have accompanied the Churches like their shadow, I need not now consider; but they are assuredly not small. If Agnostics lose heavily on the one side, they gain a good deal on the other. People who talk about the comforts of belief appear to forget its discomforts; they ignore the fact that the Christianity of the Churches is something more than faith in the ideal personality of Jesus, which they create for themselves, plus so much as can be carried into practice, without disorganizing civil society, of the maxims of the 'Sermon on the Mount'. Trip in morals or in doctrine (especially in doctrine), without due repentance or retraction, or fail to get properly baptized before you die, and a plébiscite of the Christians of Europe, if they were true to their creeds, would affirm your everlasting damnation by an immense majority.

'Agnosticism' (ibid., February 1889, reprinted ibid.)

SIR LESLIE STEPHEN
1832–1904

'Doublethink'

My own experience is, I imagine, a very common one. When I ceased to accept the teaching of my youth, it was not so much a process of giving up beliefs, as of discovering that I had never really believed. The contrast between the genuine convictions which guide and govern our conduct, and the professions which we were taught to repeat in church, when once realized, was too glaring. One belonged to the world of realities, and the other to the world of dreams. . . . The 'I believe' of the creed seemed to mean something quite different from the 'I believe' of politics and history and science. . . . (Some) have done their best to find in the Christian doctrine, rightly understood, the embodiment of the highest philosophy. It is the divine voice which speaks in our hearts, though it has caught some accretion of human passion and superstition. The popular versions are false and debased; the old versions of the Atonement, for example, monstrous; and the belief in the everlasting torture of sinners, a hideous and groundless caricature. With much that such men have said I could, of course, agree heartily; for, indeed, it expresses the strongest feelings which have caused religious revolt. But would it not be simpler to say, 'the doctrine is not true', than to say, 'it is true, but means just the reverse of what it was also taken to mean'? I prefer plain terms; and 'without doubt he shall perish everlastingly' seems to be an awkward way of denying the endlessness of punishment. You cannot denounce the immorality of the old dogmas with the infidel, and then proclaim their infinite value with the believer. You defend the doctrine by showing that in its plain downright sense,—the sense in which it embodied popular imaginations,—it was false and shocking. The proposal to hold by the words evacuated of the old meaning is a concession of the whole case to the unbeliever, and a substitution of sentiment and aspiration for a genuine intellectual belief.

'The Aims of Ethical Societies', in
***Symposium on Ethics and Religion* (1900)**

Religious Persecution

For many generations the chief Christian sects persecuted right and left; they burnt, hanged, flogged, dragonaded, enforced penal codes, drove the best part of the population into banishment, and, in short, oppressed the unfortunate minority—whichever it might be—by every conceivable instrument of tyranny. When some heretics began to denounce the practice under which they suffered, the doctrine of toleration was hooted down as savouring of Socinianism, deism, and atheism. Thanks to the rationalist spirit within and without the Churches, thanks above all to the influence of such men as Voltaire, men of all creeds have slowly come to admit that religious persecution is a detestable crime, and one of the most fruitful of all the causes of misery that depend upon the human will. And then the advocates of the Churches turn round and declare, with astonishing self-possession, that they are not responsible; persecution is quite irreconcilable with the true spirit of Christianity. If Philip II, or Louis XIV, or Henry VIII chose to persecute, so much the worse for them and their instruments. Yes; but why did you not find that out a little sooner? If I were a landlord, and had calmly sat by while my agent extorted rents from my tenants by dint of applying thumbscrews and rubbing pepper on their eyelids, am I, when my tenants have grown strong enough to turn the tables, to say quietly, 'Oh, it was quite against the letter of my instructions'? Why, then, did not I return the rents, punish the agent, and make my instructions a little plainer? And now for me, a fallible human being, substitute what you take to be the immaculate Church of God, the medium through which eternal truth is revealed to erring man; suppose that this Church profits and thrives for a time by help of the most atrocious crimes that have ever disgraced mankind; that, far from reviling the criminal, it has always denounced the victim, and now, when it is down and the victim on his legs, that it complacently observes that it was all a mistake; what am I to think of such a revelation and its God? You can damn men readily enough for not holding the right shade of belief about mysteries which you loudly proclaim to be inconceivable; did you ever—when you were strong enough—bring your tremendous arsenal of threats to bear upon men who were making a hell upon earth, and committing every abomination under the sun in your name and for your profit? You did not explicitly approve; or, rather, the persons who approved in your name did it without proper authority. But what is the good of a body which can allow its whole influence to be used in favour of unspeakable atrocities, till its power of inflicting them has vanished?

'Dreams and Realities', in
***An Agnostic's Apology and Other Essays* (1893)**

ANDREW DICKSON WHITE
1832–1918

Science and Myth

For all this dissolving away of traditional opinions regarding our sacred literature, there has been a cause far more general and powerful than any which has been given, for it is a cause surrounding and permeating all. This is simply the atmosphere of thought engendered by the development of all sciences during the last three centuries.

Vast masses of myth, legend, marvel, and dogmatic assertion, coming into this atmosphere, have been dissolved and are now dissolving quietly away like icebergs drifted into the Gulf Stream. In earlier days, when some critic in advance of his time insisted that Moses could not have written an account embracing the circumstances of his own death, it was sufficient to answer that Moses was a prophet . . . and if the discrepancy was noted between the two accounts of creation in Genesis, or between the genealogies or the dates of the crucifixion in the Gospels, the cogent reply was 'infidelity'. But the thinking world has at last been borne by the general development of a scientific atmosphere beyond that kind of refutation.

If, in the atmosphere generated by the earlier developed sciences, the older growths of biblical interpretation have drooped and withered and are evidently perishing, new and better growths have arisen with roots running down into the newer sciences, Comparative Anthropology . . . Comparative Mythology and Folklore . . . Comparative Religion and Literature. . . . While researches in these sciences have established the fact that accounts formerly supposed to be special revelations to Jews and Cristians are but repetitions of widespread legends dating from far earlier civilizations, and that beliefs formerly thought fundamental to Judaism and Christianity are simply based on ancient myths, they have also begun to impress upon the intellect and conscience of the thinking world the fact that the religious and moral truths thus disengaged from the old masses of myth and legend are all the more venerable and authoritative, and that all individual or national life of any value must be vitalized by them.

A History of the Warfare of Science with
Theology in Christendom (1876), Vol. II, Chap. XX, 6

MONCURE CONWAY
1832–1907

Freedom of Thought

Freedom of thought had gradually taken the place in my religion which freedom of the slave occupied before it was secured. Freedom of thought does not mean that a man can think and speak his honest thought without physical harm; it means that his thought and speech can be free without bringing upon him ill-will, unkindness, alienation of what is necessary to his or her happiness. It means that every honest thinker shall be the reverse of discouraged—shall be encouraged.

Apologia (1884)

We have kept together and grown in harmony and strength by the development of the religious life; by which I mean the cultivation of a love and reverence for what is morally good, for rectitude and justice, for the high ideal of life and character, for unselfishness, for the service of mankind. These things are simple. They require neither genius or learning for their discovery, but by study, by sympathy, by meditation on them day and night, these simple principles may become our delight, they may open depths of feeling and joy in ourselves, they may raise in us that most pure passion which idealises life.

Ibid.

CHARLES BRADLAUGH
1833–1891

Humanity's Gain from Unbelief

None sees a religion die; dead religions are like dead languages and obsolete customs: the decay is long and—like the glacier march—is perceptible only to the careful watcher by comparisons extending over long periods. . . .

As an unbeliever, I ask leave to plead that humanity has been a real gainer from scepticism, and that the gradual and growing rejection of Christianity—like the rejection of the faiths which preceded it—has in fact added, and will add, to man's happiness and well-being. . . .

It is customary, in controversy, for those advocating the claims of Christianity, to include all good done by men in nominally Christian countries as if such good were the result of Christianity, while they contend that the evil which exists prevails in spite of Christianity. I shall try to make out that the ameliorating march of the last few centuries has been initiated by the heretics of each age, though I quite concede that the men and women denounced and persecuted as infidels by the pious of one century are frequently claimed as saints by the pious of a later generation. . . .

Christianity and Slavery. Take one clear gain to humanity consequent on unbelief—i.e. in the abolition of slavery in some countries, in the abolition of the slave trade in most civilized countries, and in the tendency to its total abolition. I am unaware of any religion in the world which in the past forbade slavery. The professors of Christianity for ages supported it; the Old Testament repeatedly sanctioned it by special laws: the New Testament has no repealing declaration. Though we are at the close of the nineteenth century of the Christian era, it is only during the past three-quarters of a century that the battle for freedom has been gradually won. It is scarcely a quarter of a century since the famous emancipation amendment was carried to the United States Constitution. And it is impossible for any well-informed Christian to deny that the abolition movement in North America was most steadily and bitterly opposed by the religious bodies in the various States. . . .

When abolition was advocated in the United States in 1790, the representative from South Carolina was able to plead that the Southern clergy 'did not condemn either slavery or the slave trade'; and Mr. Jackson, the representative from Georgia, pleaded that 'from Genesis to Revelation' the current was favourable to slavery. Elias Hicks, the brave Abolitionist Quaker, was denounced as an atheist, and less than twenty years ago a Hicksite Quaker was expelled from one of the Southern American Legislatures because of the reputed irreligion of these abolitionist 'Friends'.

When the Fugitive Slave Law was under discussion in North America, large numbers of clergymen of nearly every denomination were found ready to defend this infamous law. Samuel James May, the famous abolitionist, was driven from the pulpit as irreligious, solely because of his attacks on slave-holding. . . .

Guizot, notwithstanding that he tries to claim that the Church exerted its influence to restrain slavery, says (*European Civilisation,* Vol. I, p. 110): 'It has often been repeated that the abolition of slavery among modern people is entirely due to Christians. That, I think, is saying too much. Slavery existed for a long period in the heart of Christian society, without its being particularly astonished or irritated. A multitude of causes, and a great development in other ideas and principles of civilization, were necessary for the abolition of this iniquity of all iniquities.' And my contention is that this 'development in other ideas and principles of civilization' was long retarded by Governments in which the Christian Church was dominant. The men who advocated liberty were imprisoned, racked, and burned, so long as the Church was strong enough to be merciless. . . .

Christianity and Witchcraft. Take further the gain to humanity consequent on the unbelief, or rather disbelief, in witchcraft and wizardry. Apart from the brutality by Christians towards those suspected of witchcraft, the hindrance to scientific initiative or experiment was incalculably great so long as belief in magic obtained. The inventions of the past two centuries, and especially those of the eighteenth century, might have benefited mankind much earlier and much more largely, but for the foolish belief in witchcraft and the shocking ferocity exhibited against those suspected of necromancy. After quoting a large number of cases of trial and punishment for witchcraft from official records in Scotland, J. M. Robertson says: 'The people seem to have passed from cruelty to cruelty precisely as they became more and more fanatical, more and more devoted to their Church, till after many generations the slow spread of human science began to counteract the ravages of superstition, the clergy resisting reason and humanity to the last. . . .' The English Statute Book under Elizabeth and under James was disfigured by enactments against witchcraft passed under pressure from the Christian Churches, which Acts have been repealed only in consequence of the disbelief in the Christian precept, 'Thou shalt not suffer a witch to live. . . .'

Mental and Bodily Disease. Is it not also fair to urge the gain to humanity which has been apparent in the wiser treatment of the insane, consequent on the unbelief in the Christian doctrine that these unfortunates were examples either of demoniacal possession or of special visitation of deity? For centuries under Christianity mental disease was most ignorantly treated. Exorcism, shackles, and the whip were the penalties rather than the curatives for mental maladies. From the heretical departure of Pinel at the close of the last century to the position of Maudsley today, every step illustrates the march of unbelief. Take the gain to humanity in the unbelief not yet complete, but now largely preponderant, in the dogma that sickness, pestilence, and famine were manifestations of divine anger, the results of which could neither be avoided nor prevented. The Christian Churches have done little or nothing to dispel this superstition. The official and authorised prayers of the principal denominations, even today, reaffirm it. Modern study of the laws of health, experiments in sanitary improvements, more careful applications of medical knowledge, have proved more efficacious in preventing or diminishing plagues and pestilence than has the intervention of the priest or the practice of prayer. . . .

Christianity and Persecution. If it stood alone it would be almost sufficient to plead as justification for heresy the approach towards equality and liberty for the utterance of all opinions achieved because of growing unbelief. At one period in Christendom each Government acted as though only one religious faith could be true, and as though the holding, or at any rate the making known, of any other opinion was a criminal act deserving punishment. Under the one word 'infidel', even as late as Lord Coke, were classed together all who were not Christians, even though they were Mohammedans, Brahmins, or Jews. . . .

Lord Coke treated the infidel as one who in law had no right of any kind, with whom no contract need be kept, to whom no debt was payable. . . . In a solemn judgment, Lord Coke says: 'All infidels are in law *perpetui inimici*; for between them, as with the devils whose subjects they be, and the Christian, there is perpetual hostility. . . .' Up till the 23rd December 1888, an infidel in Scotland was allowed to enforce any legal claim in court only on condition that, if challenged, he denied his infidelity. If he lied and said he was a Christian, he was accepted, despite his lying. If he told the truth and said he was an unbeliever, then he was practically an outlaw, incompetent to give evidence for himself or for any other. Fortunately all this was changed by the Royal assent to the Oaths Act on 24th December. Has not humanity clearly gained a little in this struggle through unbelief?

Humanity's Gain from Unbelief (1889)

ROBERT GREEN INGERSOLL
1833–1899

God and Evil

Would an infinitely wise, good, and powerful God, intending to produce man, commence with the lowest possible forms of life; with the simplest organism that can be imagined, and during immeasurable periods of time, slowly and almost impercepibly improve upon the rude beginning, until man was evolved? Would countless ages thus be wasted in the production of awkward forms, afterwards abandoned? Can the intelligence of man discover the least wisdom in covering the earth with crawling, creeping horrors, that live only upon the agonies and pangs of others? Can we see the propriety of so constructing the earth that only an insignificant portion of its surface is capable of producing an intelligent man? Who can appreciate the mercy of so making the world that all animals devour animals; so that every mouth is a slaughterhouse, and every stomach a tomb? Is it possible to discover infinite intelligence and love in universal and eternal carnage?

What would we think of a father who should give a farm to his children, and before giving them possession should plant upon it thousands of deadly shrubs and vines; should stock it with ferocious beasts and poisonous reptiles; should take pains to put a few swamps in the neighbourhood to breed malaria; should so arrange matters that the ground would occasionally open and swallow a few of his darlings; and, besides all this, should establish a few volcanoes in the immediate vicinity, that might at any moment overwhelm his children with rivers of fire? Suppose that this father neglected to tell his children which of the plants were deadly; that the reptiles were poisonous; failed to say anything about the earthquakes, and kept the volcano business a profoud secret; would we pronounce him angel or fiend? And yet this is exactly what the orthodox God has done. . . .

The Gods (1876)

A Humanist Credo

We are not endeavouring to chain the future, but to free the present. We are not forging fetters for our children, but we are breaking those our fathers made for us. We are the advocates of inquiry, of investigation and thought. This of itself is an admission that we are not perfectly satisfied with all our conclusions. Philosophy has not the egotism of faith. While superstition builds walls and creates obstructions, science opens all the highways of thought. We do not pretend to have circumnavigated everything, and to have solved all difficulties, but we do believe that it is better to love men than to fear gods; that it is grander and nobler to think and investigate for yourself than to repeat a creed. We are satisfied that there can be but little liberty on earth while men worship a tyrant in heaven. We do not expect to accomplish everything in our day; but we want to do what good we can, and to render all the service possible in the holy cause of human progress. We know that doing away with gods and supernatural persons and powers is not an end. It is a means to an end—the real end being the happiness of man. . . .

Ibid.

MARK TWAIN
1835–1910

Thoughts of God

When we reflect that the fly was not invented for pastime, but in the way of business; that he was not flung off in a heedless moment and with no object in view but to pass the time, but was the fruit of long and pains-taking labor and calculation, and with a definite and far-reaching purpose in view; that his character and conduct were planned out with cold deliberation; that his career was foreseen and foreordered, and that there was no want which he could supply, we are hopelessly puzzled, we cannot understand the moral lapse that was able to render possible the conceiving and the consummation of this squalid and malevolent creature.

Let us try to think the unthinkable; let us try to imagine a Man of a sort willing to invent the fly; that is to say, a man destitute of feeling; a man willing to wantonly torture and harass and persecute myriads of creatures who had never done him any harm and could not if they wanted to, and—the majority of them—poor dumb things not even aware of his existence. In a word, let us try to imagine a man with so singular and so lumbering a code of morals as this: that it is fair and right to send afflictions upon the just—upon the unoffending as well as upon the offending, without discrimination.

If we can imagine such a man, that is the man that could invent the fly, and send him out on his mission and furnish him his orders: 'Depart into the uttermost corners of the earth, and diligently do your appointed work. Persecute the sick child; settle upon its eyes, its face, its hands, and gnaw and pester and sting; worry and fret and madden the worn and tired mother who watches by the child, and who humbly prays for mercy and relief with the pathetic faith of the deceived and the unteachable. Settle upon the soldier's festering wounds in field and hospital and drive him frantic while he also prays, and between times curses, with none to listen but you, Fly, who get all the petting and all the protection, without even praying for it. Harry and persecute the forlorn and forsaken wretch who is perishing of the plague, and in his terror and despair praying; bite, sting, feed upon his ulcers, dabble your feet in his rotten blood, gum them thick with plague-germs—feet cunningly designed and perfected for this function ages ago in the beginning—carry this freight to a hundred tables, among the just and the unjust, the high and the low, and walk over the food and gum it with filth and death. Visit all; allow no man peace till he get it in the grave; visit and afflict the hard-worked and unoffending horse, mule, ox, ass, pester the patient cow, and all the kindly animals that labor without fair reward here and perish without hope of it hereafter; spare no creature, wild or tame; but wheresoever you find one, make his life a misery, treat him as the innocent deserve; and so please Me and increase My glory Who made the fly.'

We hear much about His patience and forbearance and long-suffering; we hear nothing about our own, which much exceeds it. We hear much about His mercy and kindness and goodness—

in words—the words of His Book and of His pulpit—and the meek multitude is content with this evidence, such as it is, seeking no further; but whoso searcheth after a concreted sample of it will in timp acquire fatigue. There being no instances of it. For what are gilded as mercies are not in any recorded case more than mere common justices, and due—due without thanks or compliment. To rescue without personal risk a cripple from a burning house is not a mercy, it is a mere commonplace duty; anybody would do it that could. And not by proxy, either—delegating the work but confiscating the credit for it. If men neglected 'God's poor' and 'God's stricken and helpless ones' as He does, what would become of them? The answer is to be found in those dark lands where man follows His example and turns his indifferent back upon them: they get no help at all; they cry, and plead and pray in vain, they linger and suffer, and miserably die. If you will look at the matter rationally and without prejudice, the proper place to hunt for the facts of His mercy, is not where man does the mercies and He collects the praise, but in those regions where He has the field to Himself.

It is plain that there is one moral law for heaven and another for the earth. The pulpit assures us that wherever we see suffering and sorrow which we can relieve and do not do it, we sin, heavily. *There was never yet a case of suffering or sorrow which God could not relieve.* Does He sin, then? It He is the Source of Morals He does—certainly nothing can be plainer than that, you will admit. Surely the Source of law cannot violate law and stand unsmirched; surely the judge upon the bench cannot forbid crime and then revel in it himself unreproached. Nevertheless we have this curious spectacle: daily the trained parrot in the pulpit gravely delivers himself of these ironies, which he has acquired at second-hand and adopted without examination, to a trained congregation which accepts them without examination, and neither the speaker nor the hearer laughs at himself. It does seem as if we ought to be humble when we are at a bench-show, and not put on airs of intellectual superiority there.

From *Thoughts of God* (early 1900s)

SAMUEL BUTLER
1835–1902

Religion

Is there any religion whose followers can be pointed to as distinctly more amiable and trustworthy than those of any other? If so, this should be enough. I find the nicest and best people generally profess no religion at all, but are ready to like the best men of all religions.

Heaven and Hell

Heaven is the work of the best and kindest men and women. Hell is the work of prigs, pedants and professional truthtellers. The world is an attempt to make the best of both.

Prayer

Prayers are to men as dolls are to children. They are not without use and comfort, but it is not easy to take them very seriously. I dropped saying mine suddenly once for all without malice prepense, on the night of the 29th of September, 1859, when I went on board the Roman Emperor to sail for New Zealand. I had said them the night before and doubted not that I was always going to say them as I always had done hitherto. That night, I suppose, the sense of change was so great that it shook them quietly off. I was not then a sceptic; I had got as far as disbelief in infant baptism but no further. I felt no compunction of conscience, however, about leaving off my morning and evening prayers—simply I could no longer say them.

Complete Death

To die completely, a person must not only forget but be forgotten, and he who is not forgotten is not dead. This is as old as *non omnis moriar* and a great deal older, but very few people realise it.

Life and Death

When I was young I used to think the only certain thing about life was that I should one day die. Now I think the only certain thing about life is that there is no such thing as death.

The Defeat of Death

There is nothing which at once affects a man so much and so little as his own death. It is a case in which the going-to-happen-ness of a thing is of greater importance than the actual thing itself which cannot be of importance to the man who dies, for Death cuts his own throat in the matter of hurting people. As a bee that can sting once but in the stinging dies, so Death is dead to him who is dead already. While he is shaking his wings, there is *brutum fulmen* but the man goes on living, frightened, perhaps, but unhurt; pain and sickness may hurt him but the moment Death strikes him both he and Death are beyond feeling. It is as though Death were born anew with every man; the two protect one another so long as they keep one another at arm's length, but if they once embrace it is all over with both.

from *Notebooks* (1912)

WILLIAM EDWARD HARTPOLE LECKY
1838–1903

Rome's Attitude towards Christianity

There can indeed, be little doubt that a chief cause of the hostility felt against the Christian Church was the intolerant aspect it at that time displayed. The Romans were prepared to tolerate almost any form of religion that would tolerate others. The Jews, though quite as obstinate as the Christians in refusing to sacrifice to the emperor, were rarely molested, except in the periods immediately following their insurrections, because Judaism, however exclusive and unsocial, was still an unaggressive national faith. But the Christian teachers taught that all religions, except their own and that of the Jews, were constructed by devils, and that all who dissented from their Church must be lost. . . . Proselytising with an untiring energy, pouring a fierce stream of invective and ridicule upon the gods on whose favour the multitude believed all national prosperity to depend, not unfrequently insulting the worshippers, and defacing the idols, they soon stung the Pagan devotees to madness, and convinced them that every calamity that fell upon the empire was the righteous vengeance of the gods. Nor was the sceptical politician more likely to regard with favour a religion whose development was plainly incompatible with the whole religious policy of the Empire. The new Church, as it was then organized, must have appeared to him essentially, fundamentally, necessarily intolerant. To permit it to triumph was to permit the extinction of religious liberty in an empire which comprised all the leading nations of the world, and tolerated all their creeds. . . . The pagan philosopher could not foresee the ghastly histories of the Inquisition, of the Albigenses, or of St. Bartholomew; but he could scarcely doubt that the Christians, when in the ascendant, would never tolerate rites which they believed to be consecrated to devils, or restrain, in the season of their power, a religious animosity which they scarcely bridled when they were weak.

History of European Morals (1877), Vol. I, Chap. III

Religious Persecution

That the Church of Rome has shed more innocent blood than any other institution that has ever existed among mankind, will be questioned by no Protestant who has a competent knowledge of history. The memorials, indeed, of many of her persecutions are now so scanty, that it is impossible to form a complete conception of the multitude of her victims, and it is quite certain that no powers of imagination can adequately realize their sufferings. Llorente, who had free access to the archives of the Spanish Inquisition, assures us that by that tribunal alone more than 31,000 persons were burnt, and more than 290,000 condemned to punishments less severe than death. The number of those who were put to death for their religion in the Netherlands alone, in the reign of Charles V, has been estimated by a very high authority at 50,000. . . . And when to these memorable instances we add the innumerable less conspicuous executions that took place, from the victims of Charlemagne to the free-thinkers of the seventeenth century, when we recollect that after the mission of Dominic the area of the persecution comprised nearly the whole of Christendom, and that its triumph was in some districts so complete as to destroy every memorial of the contest, the most callous nature must recoil with horror from the spectacle. For these atrocities were not perpetrated in the brief paroxysms of a reign of terror, or by the hands of obscure sectaries, but were inflicted by a triumphant Church, with every circumstance of solemnity and deliberation. Nor did the victims perish by a rapid and painless death, but by one which was carefully selected as among the most poignant that man can suffer. They were usually burnt alive. They were burnt alive not unfrequently by a slow fire. They were burnt alive after their constancy had been tried by the most excruciating agonies that minds fertile in torture could devise. This was the physical torment inflicted on those who dared to exercise their reason in the pursuit of truth; but what language can describe, and what imagination can conceive, the mental suffering that accompanied it? For in those days the family was divided against itself. The ray of conviction often fell upon a single member, leaving all others untouched. The victims who died for heresy were not, like those who died for witchcraft, solitary and doting women, but were usually men in the midst of active life, and often in the first flush of youthful enthusiasm, and those who loved them best were firmly convinced that their agonies upon earth were but the prelude of eternal agonies hereafter. . . . It is horrible, it is appalling to reflect what the mother, the wife, the sister, the daughter of the heretic must have suffered from this teaching. She saw the body of him who was dearer to her than life, dislocated and writhing and quivering with pain; she watched the slow fire creeping from limb to limb till it had swathed him in a sheet of agony, and when at last the scream of anguish had died away, and the tortured body was at rest, she was told that all this was acceptable to the God she served, and was but a faint image of the sufferings He would inflict through eternity upon the dead. . . . And besides all these things, we have to remember that the spirit which was manifested in acts of detailed persecution had often swept over a far wider sphere, and pro-

duced sufferings not perhaps so excruciating, but far more extensive. We have to recollect frightful massacres, perhaps the most
fearful the world has ever seen; the massacre of the Albigenses,
which a pope had instigated, or the massacre of St. Bartholomew,
for which a pope returned solemn thanks to Heaven. We have to
recollect those religious wars which reproduced themselves century after century with scarcely diminished fury, which turned
Syria into an Aceldama, which inundated with blood the fairest
lands of Europe, which blasted the prosperity and paralysed the
intellect of many a noble nation, and which planted animosities in
Europe that two hundred years have been unable altogether to
destroy. Nor should we forget the hardening effects that must
have been produced on the minds of the spectators who at every
royal marriage in Spain were regaled by the public execution of
heretics, or who were summoned to the great square of Toulouse
to contemplate the struggles of four hundred witches in the
flames. When we add together all these various forms of suffering, and estimate all their aggravations, when we think that the
victims of these persecutions were usually men who were not
only entirely guiltless, but who proved themselves by their very
deaths to be endowed with most transcendent and heroic virtues,
and when we still further consider that all this was but part of one
vast conspiracy to check the development of the human mind,
and to destroy that spirit of impartial and unrestricted inquiry
which is the very first condition of progress as of truth; when we
consider all these things, it can surely be no exaggeration to say
that the Church of Rome has inflicted a greater amount of unmerited suffering than any other religion that has ever existed among
mankind. . . .

But while the pre-eminent atrocity of the persecutions of the
Church of Rome is fully admitted, nothing can be more grossly
disingenuous or untrue than to represent persecution as her
peculiar taint. She persecuted to the full extent of the power of her
clergy, and that power was very great. The persecution of which
every Protestant Church was guilty was measured by the same
rule, but clerical influence in Protestant countries was comparatively weak. The Protestant persecutions were never so sanguinary as those of the Catholics, but the principle was affirmed
quite as strongly, was acted on quite as constantly and was

defended quite as pertinaciously by the clergy. . . . The Presbyterians through a long succession of reigns were imprisoned, branded, mutilated, scourged, and exposed in the pillory. Many Catholics under false pretences were tortured and hung. Anabaptists and Arians were burnt alive. . . . In Scotland, during nearly the whole period that the Stuarts were on the throne of England, a persecution rivalling in atrocity almost any on record was directed by the English government, at the instigation of the Scotch bishops, and with the approbation of the English Church, against all who repudiated episcopacy. . . . The Presbyterians were hunted like criminals over the mountains. Their ears were torn from the roots. They were branded with hot irons. Their fingers were wrenched asunder by the thumbkins. The bones of their legs were shattered in the boots. Women were scourged publicly through the streets. Multitudes were transported to Barbadoes, infuriated soldiers were let loose upon them, and encouraged to exercise all their ingenuity in torturing them. . . .

In Protestant Switzerland numerous Anabaptists perished by drowning; the freethinker Gentilis by the axe; Servetus, and a convert to Judaism, by the flames. In America, the colonists who were driven from their own land by persecution, not only proscribed the Catholics, but also persecuted the Quakers—the most inoffensive of all sects—with atrocious severity. If Holland was somewhat more tolerant, it was early remarked, that while the liberty allowed there was unusually great, the power accorded to the clergy was unusually small.

A History of the Rise and Influence of the Spirit of
Rationalism in Europe **(1865), Part II, Chap. IV**

JOHN MORLEY (Viscount Morley)
1838–1923

Humanist Parents and Their Children

It is possible to bring up the young in dissent from the common beliefs around them, or in indifference to them, without engendering any of that pride in eccentricity for its own sake, which is so little likeable a quality in either young or old. There is, however, little risk of an excess in this direction. The young tremble even more than the old at the penalties of nonconformity. There is more excuse for them in this. Such penalties in their case usually come closer and in more stringent forms. Neither have they had time to find out, as their elders have or ought to have found out, what a very moderate degree of fortitude enables us to bear up against social disapproval, when we know that it is nothing more than the common form of convention.

The great object is to keep the minds of the young as open as possible in the mattor of religion; to breed in them a certain simplicity and freedom from self-consciousness, in finding themselves with the religious beliefs and customs of those around them; to make them regard differences in these respects as very natural and ordinary matters, susceptible of an easy explanation. It is of course inevitable, unless they are brought up in cloistered seclusion, that they should hear much of the various articles of belief which we are anxious that they should not share. They will ask you whether the story of the creation of the universe is true; whether such and such miracles really happened; whether this person or that actually lived, and actually did all that he is said to have done. Plainly the right course is to tell them, without any agitation or excess or vehemence or too much elaboration, the simple truth in such matters exactly as it appears to one's own mind. There is no reason why they should not know the best parts of the Bible as well as they know the *Iliad* or Herodotus. There are many reasons why they should know them better. But one most important condition of this is constantly overlooked by people, who like to satisfy their intellectual vanity by scepticism, and at the same time to make their comfort safe by external conformity. If the Bible is to be taught only because it is a noble and most majestic monument of literature, it should be taught as that and no more. That a man who regards it solely as supreme literature, should impress it upon the young as the supernaturally inspired word of God and the accurate record of objective occurrences, is a piece of the plainest and most shocking dishonesty. Let a youth be trained in simple and straightforward recognition of the truth that we can know, and can conjecture, nothing with any assurance as to the ultimate mysteries of things. Let his imagination and his sense of awe be fed from those springs, which are none the less bounteous because they flow in natural rather than supernatural channels. Let him be taught the historic place and source of the religions which he is not bound to accept, unless the evidence for their authority by and by brings him to another mind. A boy or girl trained in this way has an infinitely better chance of growing up with a true spirit and learning of religion implanted in the character, than if they had been educated in formulae which they could not understand, by people who do not believe them. . . .

On Compromise (1874) **Chap. IV**

WILLIAM JAMES
1842–1910

Medical Materialism

Perhaps the commonest expression of this assumption that spiritual value is undone if lowly origin be asserted is seen in those comments which unsentimental people so often pass on their more sentimental acquaintances. Alfred believes in immortality so strongly because his temperament is so emotional. Fanny's extraordinary conscientiousness is merely a matter of overinstigated nerves. William's melancholy about the universe is due to bad digestion—probably his liver is torpid. Eliza's delight in her church is a symptom of her hysterical constitution. Peter would be less troubled about his soul if he would take more exercise in the open air, etc. A more fully developed example of the same kind of reasoning is the fashion, quite common nowadays among certain writers, of criticizing the religious emotions by showing a connection between them and the sexual life. Conversion is a crisis of puberty and adolescence. The macerations of saints, and the devotion of missionaries, are only instances of the parental instinct of self-sacrifice gone astray. For the hysterical nun, starving for natural life, Christ is but an imaginary substitute for a more earthly object of affection. And the like.

We are surely all familiar in a general way with this method of discrediting states of mind for which we have an antipathy. We all use it to some degree in criticizing persons whose states of mind we regard as overstrained, but when other people criticize our own more exalted soul-flights by calling them 'nothing but' expressions of our organic disposition, we feel outraged and hurt, for we know that, whatever be our organism's peculiarities, our mental states have their substantive value as revelations of the living truth; and we wish that all this medical materialism could be made to hold its tongue.

Medical materialism seems indeed a good appellation for the two simple-minded system of thought which we are considering. Medical materialism finishes up Saint Paul by calling his vision on the road to Damascus a discharging lesion of the occipital cortex, he being an epileptic. It snuffs out Saint Teresa as an hysteric, Saint Francis of Assisi as an hereditary degenerate. George Fox's discontent with the shams of his age, and his pining for spiritual veracity, it treats as a symptom of a disordered colon. Carlyle's organtones of misery it accounts for by a gastroduodenal catarrh. All such mental overtensions, it says, are, when you come to the bottom of the matter, mere affairs of diathesis (auto-intoxications most probably), due to the perverted action of various glands which physiology will yet discover.

It is needless to say that medical materialism draws in point of fact no such sweeping skeptical conclusion. It is sure, just as every simple man is sure, that some states of mind are inwardly superior to others, and reveal to us more truth, and in this it simply makes use of an ordinary spiritual judgment. It has no physiological theory of the production of these its favourite states, by which it may accredit them; and its attempt to discredit the states which it dislikes, by vaguely associating them with nerves and liver, and connecting them with names connoting bodily affliction, is altogether illogical and inconsistent.

Let us play fair in this whole matter, and be quite candid with ourselves and with the facts. When we think certain states of mind superior to others, is it ever because of what we know concerning their organic antecedents? No! it is always for two entirely different reasons. It is either because we take an immediate delight in them; or else it is because we believe them to bring us good consequential fruits for life. When we speak disparagingly of 'feverish fancies', surely the fever-process as such is not the ground of our disesteem—for aught we know to the contrary, 103° or 104°

Fahrenheit might be a much more favorable temperature for truths to germinate and sprout in, than the more ordinary blood-heat of 97 or 98 degrees. It is either the disagreeableness itself of the fancies, or their inability to bear the criticisms of the convalescent hour. When we praise the thoughts which health brings, health's peculiar chemical metabolisms have nothing to do with determining our judgment. We know in fact almost nothing about these metabolisms. It is the character of inner happiness in the thoughts which stamps them as good, or else their consistency with our other opinions and their service-ability for our needs, which make them pass for true in our esteem.

from the *Varieties of Religious Experience* (1902)

FRIEDRICH NIETZSCHE
1844–1900

God Is a Supposition

God is a supposition; but I want your supposing to reach no further than your creating will.

Could you create a god?—So be silent about all gods! But you could surely create the Superman.

Perhaps not you yourselves, my brothers! But you could transform yourselves into forefathers and ancestors of the Superman: and let this be your finest creating!

God is a supposition: but I want your supposing to be bounded by conceivability.

Could you conceive a god?—But may the will to truth mean this to you: that everything shall be transformed into the humanly-conceivable, the humanly-evident, the humanly-palpable! You should follow your own senses to the end!

And you yourselves should create what you have hitherto called the World: the World should be formed in your image by your reason, your will, and your love! and truly, it will be to your happiness, you enlightened men!

And how should you endure life without this hope, you enlightened men? Neither in the incomprehensible nor in the irrational can you be at home.

But to reveal my heart entirely to you, friends: if there were gods, how could I endure not to be a god! Therefore there are no gods.

I, indeed, drew that conclusion; but now it draws me.

God is a supposition: but who could imbibe all the anguish of this supposition without dying? Shall the creator be robbed of his faith and the eagle of his soaring into the heights?

God is a thought that makes all that is straight crooked and all that stands giddy. What? Would time be gone and all that is transitory only a lie?

from *Thus Spoke Zarathustra* (1883–92)

WILLIAM KINGDON CLIFFORD
1845–1879

Moral Behaviour

If I steal money from any person, there may be no harm done by the mere transfer of possession; he may not feel the loss, or it may prevent him from using the money badly. But I cannot help doing this great wrong towards Man, that I make myself dishonest. What hurts society is not that it should lose its property, but that it should become a den of thieves; for then it must cease to be society. This is why we ought not to do evil that good may come; for at any rate this great evil has come, that we have done evil and are made wicked thereby. In like manner, if I let myself believe anything on insufficient evidence, there may be no great harm done by the mere belief; it may be true after all, or I may never have occasion to exhibit it in outward acts. But I cannot help doing this great wrong towards Man, that I make myself credulous. The danger to society is not merely that it should believe wrong things, though that is great enough; but that it should become credulous, and lose the habit of testing things and inquiring into them; for then it must sink back into savagery.

from *Lectures and Essays* (1886)

Now, as we all know, there is a priesthood whose influence is not to be made light of, even in our own land, which claims to do two things; to declare with infallible authority what is right and what is wrong, and to take away the guilt of the sinner after confession has been made to it. The second of these claims we shall come back upon in connection with another part of the subject. But that claim is one which, as it seems to me, ought to condemn the priesthood making it in the eyes of every conscientious man. We must take care to keep this question to itself, and not to let it be confused with quite different ones. The priesthood in question, as we all know, has taught that as right which is not right, and has condemned as wrong some of the holiest duties of mankind. But this is not what we are here concerned with. Let us put an ideal case of a priesthood which, as a matter of fact, taught a morality agreeing with the healthy conscience of all men at a given time; but which, nevertheless, taught this as an infallible revelation. The tendency of such teaching, if really accepted, would be to destroy morality altogether, for it is of the very essence of the moral sense that it is a common perception by men of what is good for man. It arises, not in one man's mind by a flash of genius or a transport of ecstasy, but in all men's minds, as the fruit of their necessary intercourse and united labour for a common object. When an infallible authority is set up, the voice of this natural human conscience must be hushed and schooled, and made to speak the words of a formula. Obedience becomes the whole duty of man; and the notion of right is attached to a lifeless code of rules, instead of being the informing character of a nation. The natural consequence is that it fades gradually out and ends by disappearing altogether. I am not describing a purely conjectural state of things, but an effect which has actually been produced at various times and in considerable populations by the influence of the Catholic Church. It is true that we cannot find an actually crucial instance of a pure morality taught as an infallible revelation, and so in time ceasing to be morality for that reason alone. There are two circumstances which prevent this. One is that the Catholic priesthood has always practically taught an imperfect morality, and that it is difficult to distinguish between the effect of precepts which are wrong in themselves, and precepts which are only wrong because of the manner in which they are enforced. The other circumstance is that the priesthood has very rarely found a population willing to place itself completely and absolutely under priestly control. Men must live together and work for common objects even in priest-rid-den countries; and those conditions which in the course of ages have been able to create the moral sense cannot fail in some degree to recall it to men's minds and gradually to reinforce it. Thus it comes about that a great and increasing portion of life breaks free from priestly influences, and is governed upon right and rational grounds. The goodness of men shows itself in time more powerful than the wickedness of some of their religions.

Ibid.

G. W. FOOTE
1850–1915

God-making

'Man is certainly stark mad; he cannot make a flea, and yet he will be making gods by dozens!' So wrote honest Montaigne, the first great sceptic in modern history, who was so far in advance of his age that he surprised the world by venturing to doubt whether it was after all a just and sensible thing to burn a man alive for differing from his neighbours.

The history of that mental aberration which is called religion, and a survey of the present state of the world, from the fetish worshipper of central Africa to the super-subtle Theist of educated Europe, furnish us with countless illustrations of the truth of Montaigne's exclamation. God-making has always been a prevalent pastime, although it has less attraction for the modern than for the ancient mind. It was a recreation in which everyone could indulge, whether learned or illiterate, young or old, rich or poor. All the material needed to fashion gods of was ignorance, and there was always an unlimited stock of that article. The artificer was imagination, a glorious faculty, which is the highest dower of the creative artist and the scientific discoverer, and in their service is fruitful in usefulness and beauty, but which in the service of theology is a frightful curse, filling the mental world with fantastic monsters who waylay and devour.

Common people, however, who did the work of the world, were not able to do much god-making. Their leisure and ability were both limited. But they had a large capacity for admiring the productions of others, and their deficiencies were supplied by a special class of men, called priests, who were set apart for the manufacture of deities, and who devoted their time and their powers to the holy trade. This pious division of labour, this specialisation of function, still continues. Carpenters and tailors, grocers and butchers, who are immersed all the week in labour or business, have no opportunity for long excursions in the field of divinity; and therefore they take their religion at second hand from the priest on Sunday. It was not the multitude, but the sacred specialists, who built up the gigantic and elaborate edifice of theology, which is a purely arbitrary construction, deriving all its design and coherence from the instinctive logic of the human mind, that operates alike in a fairy tale and in a syllogism.

from *Flowers of Freethought* (1886)

SIGMUND FREUD
1856–1939

Religion and Illusion

If after this survey (of the nature of illusions and delusions) we turn again to religious doctrines, we may reiterate that they are all illusions, they do not admit of proof, and no one can be compelled to consider them as true or to believe in them. Some of them are so improbable, so very incompatible with everything we have laboriously discovered about the reality of the world, that we may compare them—taking adequately into account the psychological differences—to delusions. Of the reality value of most of them we cannot judge; just as they cannot be proved, neither can they be refuted. We still know too little to approach them critically. The riddles of the universe only reveal themselves slowly to our enquiry, to many questions science can as yet give no answer; but scientific work is our only way to the knowledge of external reality. Again, it is merely illusion to expect anything from intuition or trance; they can give us nothing but particulars, which are difficult to interpret, about our own mental life, never information about the questions that are so lightly answered by the doctrines of religion. It would be wanton to let one's one arbitrary action fill the gap, and according to one's personal estimate declare this or that part of the religious system to be more or less acceptable. These questions are too momentous for that; too sacred, one might say.

At this point it may be objected: well, then, if even the crabbed sceptics admit that the statements of religion cannot be confuted by reason, why should not I believe in them, since they have so much on their side—tradition, the concurrence of mankind, and all the consolation they yield? Yes, why not? Just as no one can be forced into belief so no one can be forced into unbelief. But do not deceive yourself into thinking that with such arguments you are following the path of correct reasoning. If ever there was a case of facile argument, this is one. Ignorance is ignorance; no right to believe anything is derived from it. No reasonable man will behave so frivolously in other matters or rest content with such feeble grounds for his opinions or for the attitude he adopts; it is only in the highest and holiest things that he allows this. In reality these are only attempts to delude oneself or other people into the belief that one still holds fast to religion, when one has long cut oneself loose from it. Where questions of religion are concerned people are guilty of every possible kind of insincerity and intellectual misdemeanour. Philosophers stretch the meaning of words until they retain scarcely anything of their original sense; by calling 'God' some vague abstraction which they have created for themselves, they pose as deists, as believers, before the world; they may even pride themselves on having attained a higher and purer idea of God, although their God is nothing but an insubstantial shadow and no longer the mighty personality of religious doctrine. Critics persist in calling 'deeply religious' a person who confesses to a sense of man's insignificance and impotence in face of the universe, although it is not this feeling that constitutes the essence of religious emotion, but rather the next step, the reaction to it, which seeks a remedy against this feeling. He who goes no further, he who humbly acquiesces in the insignificant part man plays in the universe, is, on the contrary, irreligious in the truest sense of the word.

The Future of an Illusion (1927), Chap. VI,
trans. W. D. Robson-Scott

Education for Reality

And so I disagree with you when you go on to argue that man cannot in general do without the consolation of the religious illusion, that without it he would not endure the troubles of life, the cruelty of reality. Certainly this is true of the man into whom you have instilled the sweet—or bitter-sweet—poison from childhood on. But what of the other, who has been brought up soberly? Perhaps he, not suffering from neurosis, will need no intoxicant to deaden it. True, man will then find himself in a difficult situation. He will have to confess his utter helplessness and his insignificant part in the working of the universe; he will have to confess that he is no longer the centre of creation, no longer the object of the tender care of a benevolent providence. He will be in the same position as the child who has left the home where he was so warm and comfortable. But, after all, is it not the destiny of childishness to be overcome? Man cannot remain a child for ever; he must venture at last into the hostile world. This may be called '*education to reality*'; need I tell you that it is the sole aim of my book to draw attention to the necessity for this advance?

You fear, probably, that he will not stand the test? Well, anyhow, let us be hopeful. It is at least something to know that one is thrown on one's own resources. One learns then to use them properly. And man is not entirely without means of assistance; since the time of the deluge science has taught him much, and it will still further increase his power. And as for the great necessities of fate, against which there is no remedy, these he will simply learn to endure with resignation. Of what use to him is the illusion of a kingdom on the moon, whose revenues have never yet been seen by anyone? As an honest crofter on this earth he will know how to cultivate his plot in a way that will support him. Thus by withdrawing his expectations from the other world and concentrating all his liberated energies on this earthly life he will probably attain to a state of things in which life will be tolerable for all and no one will be oppressed by culture any more.

You shall not find me impervious to your criticism. I know how difficult it is to avoid illusion; perhaps even the hopes I have confessed to are of an illusory nature. But I hold fast to one distinction. My illusions—apart from the fact that no penalty is imposed for not sharing them—are not, like the religious ones, incapable of correction, they have no delusional character. If experience should show—not to me, but to others after me who think as I do—that we are mistaken, then we shall give up our expectations. Take my endeavour for what it is. A psychologist, who does not deceive himself about the difficulty of finding his bearings in this world, strives to review the development of mankind in accord with what insight he has won from studying the mental processes of the individual during his development from childhood to manhood. In this connection the idea forces itself upon him that religion is comparable to a childhood neurosis, and he is optimistic enough to assume that mankind will overcome this neurotic phase, just as so many children grow out of their similar neuroses. These pieces of knowledge from individual psychology may be inadequate, their application to the human race justified, the optimism without foundation; I grant you the uncertainty of all these things. But often we cannot refrain from saying what we think, excusing ourselves on the ground that it is given for no more than it is worth.

And there are two points that I must dwell on a little longer. First, the weakness of my position does not betoken any strengthening of yours. I think you are defending a lost cause. We may insist as much as we like that the human intellect is weak in comparison with human instincts, and be right in doing so. But nevertheless there is something peculiar about this weakness. The voice of the intellect is a soft one, but it does not rest until it has gained a hearing. Ultimately, after endlessly repeated rebuffs, it succeeds. This is one of the few points in which one may be optimistic about the future of mankind, but in itself it signifies not a little. And one can make it a starting-point for yet other hopes. The primacy of the intellect certainly lies in the far, far, but still probably not infinite, distance; And as it will presumably set itself the same aims that you expect to be realized by your God—of course within human limits, in so far as external reality,' *Ananke* [necessity], allows it—the brotherhood of man and the reduction of suffering, we may say that our antagonism is only a temporary and not an irreconcilable one. We desire the same things, but you are more impatient, more exacting, and—why should I not say it—more selfish than I and those like me. You would have the state of bliss to begin immediately after death; you ask of it the impossible, and you will not surrender the claim of the individual. Of these wishes our god *Logos* [reason] will realize those which external nature permits, but he will do this very gradually, only in the incalculable future and for other children of men. Compensation for us, who suffer grievously from life, he does not promise. On the way to this distant goal your religious doctrines will have to be discarded, no matter whether the first attempts fail, or whether the first substitute-formations prove to be unstable. You know why; in the long run nothing can withstand reason and experience, and the contradiction religion offers to both is only too palpable. Not even the purified religious ideas can escape this fate, so long as they still try to preserve anything of the consolation of religion. Certainly if you confine yourself to the belief in a higher spiritual being, whose qualities are indefinable and whose intentions cannot be discerned, then you are proof against the interference of science, but then you will also relinquish the interest of men.

And secondly: note the difference between your attitude to illusions and mine. You have to defend the religious illusion with all your might; if it were discredited—and to be sure it is sufficiently menaced—then your world would collapse, there would be nothing left for you but to despair of everything, of culture and of the future of mankind. From this bondage I am, we are, free. Since we are prepared to renounce a good part of our infantile wishes, we can bear it if some of our expectations prove to be illusions.

Ibid., Chaps. IX, X

JOHN DEWEY
1859–1952

Mystical Experience

A region that is claimed by religionists as a special reserve . . . is mystical experience. The difference, however, between mystic experience and the theory about it that is offered to us must be noted. The experience is a fact to be inquired into. The theory, like any theory, is an interpretation of the fact. The idea that by its very nature the experience is a veridical realization of the direct presence of God does not rest so much upon examination of the facts as it does upon importing into their interpretation a conception that is formed outside them. In its dependence upon a prior conception of the supernatural, which is the thing to be proved, it begs the question.

History exhibits many types of mystic experience, and each of these types is contemporaneously explained by the concepts that prevail in the culture and the circle in which the phenomena occur. There are mystic crises that arise, as among some North American Indian tribes, induced by fasting. They are accompanied by trances and semi-hysteria. Their purpose is to gain some special power, such perhaps as locating a person who is lost or finding objects that have been secreted. There is the mysticism of Hindoo practice now enjoying some vogue in Western countries. There is the mystic ecstasy of Neo-platonism with its complete abrogation of the self and absorption into an impersonal whole of Being. There is the mysticism of intense aesthetic experience independent of any theological or metaphysical interpretation. There is the heretical mysticism of William Blake. . . .

There is no reason for denying the existence of experiences that are called mystical. On the contrary, there is every reason to suppose that, in some degree of intensity, they occur so frequently that they may be regarded as normal manifestations. . . . Yet the mystic experience yields, as we have seen, various results in the way of belief to different persons, depending upon the surrounding culture of those who undergo it. As a method, it lacks the public character belonging to the method of intelligence. Moreover, when the experience in question does not yield consciousness of the presence of God, in the sense that is alleged to exist, the retort is always at hand that it is not a genuine religious experience. For by definition only that experience is religious which arrives at this particular result. The argument is circular. The traditional position is that some hardness or corruption of heart prevents one from having the experience. Liberal religionists are now more humane. But their logic does not differ. . . .

A Common Faith (1934), Chap. II

Science versus Dogma

Apologists for a religion often point to the shift that goes on in scientific ideas and materials as evidence of the unreliability of science as a mode of knowledge. They often seem peculiarly elated by the great, almost revolutionary, change in fundamental physical conceptions that has taken place in science during the present generation. Even if the alleged unreliability were as great as they assume (or even greater), the question would remain: Have we any other recourse for knowledge? But in fact they miss the point. Science is not constituted by any particular body of subject-matter. It is constituted by a method, a method of changing beliefs by means of tested inquiry as well as of arriving at them. It is its glory, not its condemnation, that its subject-matter develops as the method is improved. There is no special subject-matter of belief that is sacrosanct. The identification of science with a particular set of beliefs and ideas is itself a hold-over of ancient and still current dogmatic habits of thought which are opposed to science In Its actuality and which science is undermining.

For scientific method is adverse not only to dogma but to doctrine as well, provided we take 'doctrine' in its usual meaning—a body of definite beliefs that need only to be taught and learned as true. This negative attitude of science to doctrine does not indicate indifference to truth. It signifies supreme loyalty to the method by which truth is attained. The scientific-religious conflict ultimately is a conflict between allegiance to this method and allegiance to even an irreducible minimum of belief so fixed in advance that it can never be modified.

Ibid.

JOHN BAGNALL BURY
1861–1927

Freedom of Speech

The progress of civilization, if it is partly conditioned by circumstances beyond man's control, depends more, and in an increasing measure, on things which are within his own power. Prominent among these are the advancement of knowledge and the deliberate adaptation of his habits and institutions to new conditions. To advance knowledge and to correct errors, unrestricted freedom of discussion is required. History shows that knowledge grew when speculation was perfectly free in Greece, and that in modern times, since restrictions on inquiry have been entirely removed, it has advanced with a velocity which would seem diabolical to the slaves of the mediaeval Church. Then, it is obvious that in order to readjust social customs, institutions, and methods to new needs and circumstances, there must be unlimited freedom of canvassing and criticizing them, of expressing the most unpopular opinions, no matter how offensive to prevailing sentiment they may be. If the history of civilization has any lesson to teach it is this: there is one supreme condition of mental and moral progress which it is completely within the power of man himself to secure, and that is perfect liberty of thought and discussion. The establishment of this liberty may be considered the most valuable achievement of modern civilization, and as a condition of social progress it should be deemed fundamental. The considerations of permanent utility on which it rests must outweigh any calculations of present advantage which from time to time might be thought to demand its violation. . . .

Meanwhile nothing should be left undone to impress upon the young that freedom of thought is an axiom of human progress. It may be feared, however, that this is not likely to be done for a long time to come. For our methods of early education are founded on authority. It is true that children are sometimes exhorted to think for themselves. But the parent or instructor who gives this excellent advice is confident that the results of the child's thinking for himself will agree with the opinions which his elders consider desirable. It is assumed that he will reason from principles which have already been instilled into him by authority. But if his thinking for himself takes the form of questioning these principles, whether moral or religious, his parents and teachers, unless they are very exceptional persons, will be extremely displeased, and will certainly discourage him. It is, of course, only singularly promising children whose freedom of thought will go so far. In this sense it might be said that 'distrust thy father and mother' is the first commandment with promise. It should be a part of education to explain to children, as soon as they are old enough to undersand, when it is reasonable, and when it is not, to accept what they are told, on authority.

A History of Freedom of Thought (1913), Chap. VIII

GOLDWORTHY LOWES DICKINSON
1862–1932

Greek Ethics

As with the excellence of the body, so with that of the soul, the conception that dominated the mind of the Greeks was primarily aesthetic. In speaking of their religion we have already remarked that they had no sense of sin; and we may now add that they had not what we are apt to mean by a sense of duty. Moral virtue they conceived not as obedience to an external law, a sacrifice of the natural man to a power that in a sense is alien to himself, but rather as the tempering into due proportion of the elements of which human nature is composed. . . . 'Virtue', says Plato, 'will be a kind of health and beauty and good habit of the soul; and vice will be a disease and deformity and sickness of it.[1]

This conception of virtue we find expressed in many forms, but always with the same underlying idea. A favourite watchword with the Greeks is the 'middle' or 'mean' the exact point of rightness between two extremes. 'Nothing in excess' was a motto inscribed over the temple of Delphi; and none could be more characteristic of the ideal of these lovers of proportion. Aristotle, indeed, has made it the basis of his whole theory of ethics. In his conception, virtue is the mean, vice the excess lying on either side—courage, for example, the mean between foolhardiness and cowardice, temperance, between incontinence and insensibility, generosity, between extravagance and meanness. The various phases of feeling and the various kinds of action he analyses minutely on this principle, understanding always by 'the mean' that which adapts itself in the due proportion to the circumstances and requirements of every case. . . .

The idea thus formulated by Aristotle is typically Greek. In another form it is the basis of the ethical philosophy of Plato, who habitually regards virtue as a kind of 'order'. . . . The view, as we said at the beginning, is properly aesthetic rather than moral. It regards life less as a battle between two contending principles . . . than as the maintenance of a balance between elements neutral in themselves but capable, according as their relations are rightly ordered or the reverse, or producing either that harmony which is called virtue, or that discord which is called vice.

Such being the conception of virtue characteristic of the Greeks, it follows that the motive to pursue it can hardly have presented itself to them in the form of what we call the 'sense of duty'. For duty emphasizes self-repression. Against the desires of man it sets a law of prohibition, a law which is not conceived as that of his own complete nature, asserting against a partial or disproportioned development the balance and totality of the ideal, but rather as a rule imposed from without by a power distinct from himself, for the mortification, not the perfecting, of his natural impulses and aims. Duty emphasizes self-repression; the Greek view emphasized self-development. . . .

From all this it follows clearly enough that the Greek ideal was far removed from asceticism; but it might perhaps be supposed, on the other hand, that it came dangerously near to licence. . . . That there were libertines among the Greeks, as everywhere else, goes without saying; but the conception that the Greek rule of life was to follow impulse and abandon restraint is a figment of would-be 'Hellenists' of our own time. The word which best sums up the ideal of the Greeks is 'temperance';the mean', 'order', 'harmony', as we saw, are its characteristic expressions; and the self-realization to which they aspired was not an anarchy of passion, but an ordered evolution of the natural faculties under the strict control of a balanced mind.

The Greek View of Life (1896), Chap. III, 5, 6

1. *Republic,* 444, trans. Davis and Vaughan.

GEORGE GILBERT AIMÉ MURRAY
1866–1957

'Doublethink'

(Many profess religious belief) not quite because they believe it to be true, but because they are strongly convinced that it is good for other people to believe it; that in fact average human nature cannot get on without it.

The adherents of this line of thought inevitably find themselves confronted by a well-known problem: their creed, however it is expressed, means something quite different to the educated thinker and to the unthinking multitude. Cicero himself held the office of Augur: he considered it of the utmost importance that the Roman people should continue to observe the traditional pieties and sanctities of the Roman religion; he duly performed the rites and took the auspices. Yet . . . he quotes with approval Cato's expression of wonder that two *haruspices* can look each other in the face without laughing.[1] The priests of the modern Roman Church when presiding over certain miracles in the South of Italy may well feel the same difficulty as the *haruspices* did, and no doubt surmount it as successfully. So much most people will admit. But the position of that eminent and high-minded body of men, the Board Church leaders of the nineteenth century, is open to a very similar criticism. Dr. Bridges in one of his essays[2] quotes certain passages from Dr. Jowett's thoughts on religion; for example: 'Limits of change within the Christian religion. The conception of miracles may become impossible and absurd. Immortality may pass into present consciousness of goodness and of God. The personality of God may pass into an idea. Doctrines may become unmeaning words.' And a little later: 'Christianity has become one religion among many. . . . We pray to God as a person; but there must always be a *subintelligitur* that He is not a person. Our forms of worship, public and private, imply some interference with the course of Nature, (yet) we know that the empire of law permeates all things.' Dr. Jowett's High Church critics found it easy to argue that such doctrines, or rather such radical scepticisms, were inconsistent not merely with the Articles of Faith which Dr. Jowett had signed, but with the obvious implications of his position as a clergyman of the Established Church. His defence, that he was assisting in a vital movement for the liberalizing and enlightening of the Church, is a strong one, but not for the moment relevant to our discussion. It is clear that in these creeds with a *subintelligitur* attached, we are not far from the position attributed by Gibbon to the cultivated circles in ancient Rome, that all religions were to the uneducated equally true, to the philosopher equally false, and to the statesman equally useful. A position which has a great deal to be said for it, but which cannot satisfy a speculative mind determined to preserve its honesty as well as its religious emotion.

'**What Is Permanent Positivism**' in
Stoic, Christian and Humanist (1940)

1. *De Divinatione*, ii, 51
2. *Illustrations of Positivism*, pp. 64 ff.

Wishful Thinking and Anthropomorphism

(Despite the many) changes in the conceptions man has formed of the God or gods of his worship, he never really gets away from either his man-thinking or his wish-thinking. In our own day it seems to me that both are being reemphasized. The ordinary Christian apologist has almost forgotten to argue that his creed is true; he concentrates so exclusively on arguing that it is a comfort, a source of good life, a psychological necessity: in fact that the only way to be happy is to believe it, or perhaps not so much to believe it, but to accept and act upon it. That is confessedly wish-thinking. And at the same time there is a revival of extreme man-thinking in reaction against the impersonal theisms of philosophers like Green and Bradley, Kant and Spinoza. Emphasis is laid, not merely in evangelical circles but much more widely, on the worship of the man-god Jesus and the intimate personal relation which his worshippers claim to have established with him as with a human friend.

Is it possible to rid ourselves of these two weaknesses, man-thinking and wish-thinking, and yet retain any effective conception of God? I doubt it. A certain Arab mystic has made the trenchant criticism that to call God 'righteous' implies just as profound anthropomorphism as to say that he has a beard. 'He is just', 'He is merciful', 'He is long-suffering', 'He loves mankind' . . . all such phrases apply to God human qualities and human ways of behaviour. Take them away, and you are left with some purely abstract residuum, indescribable and inconceivable: not even a Reason or an Intelligence or a Purpose, for each of these is essentially a human thing, an attribute of a limited being who has to think, plan and take pains. I see no escape from the conclusion that if you take away the humanity of God, you take away the traditional conception of God altogether.

Ibid.

Man a Social Animal

The whole supposition that a system of violent and intense rewards and punishments is necessary to induce human beings to perform acts for the good of others is based on a false psychology which starts from the individual isolated man instead of man the social animal. Man is an integral member of his group. Among his natural instincts there are those which aim at group-preservation as well as self-preservation; at the good of *autrui* as well as of *moi*. Even among the animals, a cow, a tigress, a hen pheasant, does not need a promise of future rewards to induce her to risk her life to save her young from harm. The male bison or gorilla needs no reward before fighting devotedly for his females and children. They all instinctively care for *autrui*. And it would be a mistake to imagine that this devotion only shows itself in the form of fighting, or only in dangerous crises. It is part of the daily life of any natural group or herd: the strong members help the weak, the weak run for protection to the strong. In man even in his primitive state these instincts are much more highly developed than in the gregarious animals; with the process of civilization they increase in range, in reasonableness, in sublimity. In the late war, how many thousands of men—not particularly selected or highminded men—risked their lives eagerly to save a companion wounded in No Man's Land? They did not ask or know why they did it. Some may have alleged motives of religion, or motives of ambition in the form of medals or promotions. But the basic motive was probably more or less the same all through; that instinctively they could not see a mate lying there wounded and not try to help him.

Ibid.

CHAPMAN COHEN
1868–1954

Christianity and Social Ethics

Far from Christianity presenting us with an adequate social ethic, it is positively deficient in both a rational conception of the nature of morality and of the conditions of its development. The mere enunciation of superficially attractive moral precepts does not—to modern minds, at least—constitute a man a great moral teacher. . . . Moreover, general precepts of the nature of those attributed to Jesus . . . are necessarily vague in character, and correspondingly useless in practice. To be of use we require with such precepts some rule of interpretation that would allow of their application to the changing circumstances of a developing society. To love one's neighbour as one's self may be a good enough rule, but its value will depend upon the circumstances determining its application. Christians who made the dungeon and the stake the reward of heresy were often enough convinced that they were acting in the best interests of their neighbours in seeking to enforce uniformity of belief upon all. So, too, with such a teaching as 'The labourer is worthy of his hire'. One cannot well conceive anyone disagreeing with this: and the agreement robs it of all practical value. What is needed is not the vague counsel that he who labours should receive adequate payment, but some equitable rule of determining what the social value of labour really is. The truth is that such precepts were never intended to apply to such social problems as confront modern society, and therefore they break down with any attempt to apply them. . . .

The great fault of all Christian teaching and of Christian teachers have been the assumption that morality can develop without appropriate material and social conditions. Morality has been treated as though it existed *in vacuo*. (Even marriage and family life tend to have been regarded as drags on spiritual progress, to be tolerated rather than encouraged.)

Nothing was further from the minds of primitive Christians than social reform; nothing more foreign to the whole of the New Testament than a political philosophy. That the State—in the sense of the entire social structure—could be, and in fact is, the great determinant in the life of man, is a view of things never once reached by the New Testament writers. The individual is addressed as an individual, not as a member of an organic whole. Yet in any really scientific view of the case general individual improvement is to be realized through social life, or not at all. . . . Such a conception is, however, quite foreign to the New Testament, as is also that of a sense of obligation to the public at large. In this respect Christian ethics is much inferior to pagan teaching. . . .

The only form in which Christianity encountered a labour problem in early times was in the form of the question of slavery. And with what result? In all the recorded utterances of the Gospel Jesus, there is not a single condemnation of slavery as an institution. In the Pagan world the question of the legitimacy of slavery was already beginning to excite interest; slaves themselves were exhibiting symptoms of unrest; but the Gospel Jesus appears oblivious to their existence. Further, we find St. Paul sending back a runaway slave to his master, and commanding slaves (wrongly translated 'servants' in the English New Testament) to be obedient to their masters, in fear and trembling, whether they be good or bad, and to count them as being 'worthy of all honour' whether the masters be believers or unbelievers; while to bear unmerited punishment in silence and patience is to be counted to their honour hereafter. . . .

The modern black-slave trade, it must also be noted, was pre-eminently a Christian traffic—instituted by Christians, and at a time when the supremacy of Christianity was practically unquestioned. And it remained, backed up by Christians, who quoted the New Testament and 'the pure Christianity of Apostolic times' as their authorities, until the writings of Thomas Paine, with the perception that free labour was economically more advantageous than forced tabour, led to its abolition. And the glaring fact remains that no Christian country has ever abolished slavery while its continuance was economically profitable. Thus an examination of the one point on which both the teaching and influence of Christianity on the position of the poor could be decisively tested, results in an emphatic condemnation.

A defence of Christian morality is often attempted, not from the standpoint of direct teaching, but from that of its sympathy with weakness and suffering, and the spirit of compassion it has evoked. Now no one, so far as I am aware, has any complaint to make against sympathy with suffering, or with the desire to help such as fall by the way in the struggle of life. . . . But the point of my criticism against Christianity is that, by its lack of desirable social teaching and intellectual discipline, it has tended to make sympathy with suffering maudlin and injurious instead of sane and helpful. Had Christianity merely taught kindness towards the unfortunate, criticism would have been impossible. But it has done more. It has glorified weakness and suffering, and held them up as necessary elements in an ideal character. It has taught people to be patient under wrong and oppression, where a preaching of discontent would have been far more helpful. It has preached patience—not the patience that results from the stern resolve to bear the inevitable with courage, but the patience that recognizes in misery the work of an all-powerful providence whose decrees it is blasphemy to question. Patience of the former kind may have its uses; patience of the latter and Christian kind only makes the continued existence of wrong the more certain.

All that Christian teaching has ever done is, at most, to make the lot of the sufferer a little more tolerable. But, so far as our sympathies lead to this, without our knowledge causing us to essay the task of preventing the perpetuation of evil social conditions . . our sympathies tend to become our deadliest enemies instead of our best friends. . . .

From thousands of pulpits (Christianity) has preached that pain develops character, that suffering sweetens and ennobles life. They do nothing of the kind. They deaden and degrade. . . . This teaching has been a useful one for the few whose power has been consolidated by its acceptance; it has been a disastrous teaching for the many. By its influence the public conscience has been deadened to the existence of the mass of removable misery in its midst. Christian sympathy may have made its existence bearable; a healthy intelligence would have made its continuance an impossibility.

***Christianity and Ethics* (1945)**

BERTRAND ARTHUR WILLIAM RUSSELL (EARL RUSSELL)
1872–1970

Religion and Fear

Fear is the basis of religious dogma, as of so much else in human life. Fear of human beings, individually or collectively, dominates much of our social life, but it is fear of nature that gives rise to religion. The antithesis of mind and matter is, as we have seen, more or less illusory; but there is another antithesis which is more important—that, namely, between things that can be affected by our desires, and things that cannot be so affected. The line between the two is neither sharp nor immutable—as science advances, more and more things are brought under human control. Nevertheless there remain things definitely on the other side. Among these are all the large facts of our world, the sort of facts that are dealt with by astronomy. It is only facts on or near the surface of the earth that we can, to some extent, mould to suit our desires. And even on the surface of the earth our powers are very limited. Above all, we cannot prevent death, although we can often delay it.

Religion is an attempt to overcome this antithesis. If the world is controlled by God, and God can be moved by prayer, we acquire a share in omnipotence. In former days, miracles happened in answer to prayer; they still do in the Catholic Church, but Protestants have lost this power. However, it is possible to dispense with miracles, since Providence has decreed that the operation of natural laws shall produce the best possible results. Thus belief in God still serves to humanize the world of nature, and to make men feel that physical forces are really their allies. In like manner immortality removes the terror from death. People who believe that when they die they will inherit eternal bliss may be expected to view death without horror, though, fortunately for medical men, this does not invariably happen. It does, however, soothe men's fears somewhat even when it cannot allay them wholly.

Religion, since it has its source in terror, has dignified certain kinds of fear, and made people think them not disgraceful. In this it has done mankind a great disservice: all fear is bad. I believe that when I die I shall rot, and nothing of my ego will survive. I am not young, and I love life. But I should scorn to shiver with terror at the thought of annihilation. Happiness is none the less true happiness because it must come to an end, nor do thought and love lose their value because they are not everlasting. Many a man has borne himself proudly on the scaffold; surely the same pride should teach us to think truly about man's place in the world. Even if the open windows of science at first make us shiver after the cosy indoor warmth of traditional humanizing myths, in the end the fresh air brings vigour, and the great spaces have a splendour of their own.

What I Believe (1925), reprinted in
Why I am Not a Christian and Other Essays (1957)

The Happy Man

It should be our endeavour . . . to aim at avoiding self-centred passions and at acquiring those affections and those interests which will prevent our thoughts from dwelling perpetually upon ourselves. It is not the nature of most men to be happy in a prison, and the passions which shut us up in ourselves constitute one of the worst kinds or prisons. Among such passions some of the commonest are fear, envy, the sense of sin, self-pity and self-admiration. In all these our desires are centred upon ourselves: there is no genuine interest in the outer world, but only a concern lest it should in some way injure us or fail to feed our ego. . . .

The happy life is to an extraordinary extent the same as the good life. Professional moralists have made too much of self-denial, and in so doing have put the emphasis in the wrong place. Conscious self-denial leaves a man self-absorbed, and vividly aware of what he has sacrificed. . . . What is needed is not self-denial, but that kind of direction of interest outward which will lead spontaneously and naturally to the same acts that a person absorbed in the pursuit of his own virtue could only perform by means of conscious self-denial.

There is another difference, somewhat more subtle, between the attitude towards life that I have been recommending and that which is recommended by the traditional moralists. The traditional moralist, for example, will say that love should be unselfish. In a certain sense he is right, that is to say, it should not be selfish beyond a point, but it should undoubtedly be of such a nature that one's own happiness is bound up in its success. If a man were to invite a lady to marry him on the ground that he ardently desired her happiness and at the same time considered that she would afford him ideal opportunities of self-abnegation, I think it may be doubted whether she would be altogether pleased. Undoubtedly we should desire the happiness of those whom we love, but not as an alternative to our own. In fact the whole antithesis between self and the rest of the world, which is implied in the doctrine of self-denial, disappears as soon as we have any genuine interest in persons or things outside ourselves. Through such interests a man comes to feel himself part of the stream of life, not a hard separate entity like a billiard ball, which can have no relation with other such entities except that of collision. . . . The happy man is the man . . . whose personality is neither divided against itself nor pitted against the world. Such a man feels himself a citizen of the universe, enjoying freely the spectacle that it offers, and the joys that it affords, untroubled by the thought of death because he feels himself not really separate from those who will come after him. It is in such profound instinctive union with the stream of life that the greatest joy is to be found.

The Conquest of Happiness (1930), Chap. XVII

The Faith of a Humanist

When I try to discover what are the original sources of my opinions, both practical and theoretical, I find that most of them spring ultimately from admiration for two qualities—kindly feeling and veracity. To begin with kindly feeling: most of the social and political evils of the world arise through absence of sympathy and presence of hatred, envy, or fear. . . . Every kind of hostile action or feeling provokes a reaction by which it is increased and so generates a progeny of violence and injustice which has a terrible vitality. This can only be met by cultivating in ourselves and attempting to generate in the young feelings of friendliness rather than hostility, of well-wishing rather than malevolence, and of co-operation rather than competition.

If I am asked 'Why do you believe this?' I should not appeal to any supernatural authority, but only to the general wish for happiness. A world full of hate is a world full of sorrow. From the point of view of worldly wisdom, hostile feeling and limitation of sympathy are folly. Their fruits are war, death, oppression, and torture, not only for their original victims but, in the long run, also for their perpetrators or their descendants. Whereas if we could all learn to love our neighbours the world would quickly become a paradise for us all.

Veracity, which I regard as second only to kindly feeling, consists broadly in believing according to evidence and not because a belief is comfortable or a source of pleasure. In the absence of veracity, kindly feeling will often be defeated by self-deception. . . . Veracity, or love of truth, is defined by Locke as 'not entertaining any proposition with greater assurance than the proofs it is built upon will warrant. This definition is admirable in regard to all those matters as to which proof may reasonably be demanded. But since proofs need premises, it is impossible to prove anything unless some things are accepted without proof. We must therefore ask ourselves: What sort of thing is it reasonable to believe with proof? I should reply: The facts of sense-experience and the principles of mathematics and logic—including the inductible logic employed in science. These are things which we can hardly bring ourselves to doubt and as to which there is a large measure of agreement among mankind. But in matters as to which men disagree, or as to which our own convictions are wavering, we should look for proofs, or, if proofs cannot be found, we should be content to confess ignorance.

There are some who hold that veracity should have limitations. Some beliefs, they say, are both comforting and morally beneficial, although it cannot be said that there are valid scientific grounds for supposing them to be true; these beliefs, they say, should not be critically examined. I cannot myself admit any such doctrine. I cannot believe that mankind can be the better for shrinking from the examination of this or that question. No sound morality can need to be based upon evasion, and a happiness derived from beliefs not justified on any ground except their pleasantness is not a kind of happiness that can be unreservedly admired.

These considerations apply especially to religious beliefs. Most of us have been brought up to believe that the universe owes its existence to an all-wise and all-powerful Creator, whose purposes are beneficent even in what to us may seem evil. I do not think it is right to refuse to apply to this belief the kind of tests that we should apply to one that touches our emotions less intimately and profoundly. Is there any evidence of the existence of such a Being? Undoubtedly belief in Him is comforting and sometimes has some good moral effects on character and behaviour. But this is no evidence that the belief is true. For my part, I think the belief lost whatever rationality it once possessed when it was discovered that the earth is not the centre of the universe. So long as it was thought that the sun and the planets and the stars revolved about the earth, it was natural to suppose that the universe had a purpose connected with the earth, and, since man was what man most admired on the earth, this purpose was supposed to be embodied in man. But astronomy and geology have changed all this. The earth is a minor planet of a minor star which is one of many millions of stars in a galaxy which is one of many millions of galaxies. Even within the life of our own planet man is only a brief interlude. Non-human life existed for countless ages before man was evolved. Man, even if he does not commit scientific suicide, will perish ultimately through failure of water or air or warmth. It is difficult to believe that Omnipotence needed so vast a setting for so small and transitory a result. . . .

There is a different and vaguer conception of cosmic Purpose as not omnipotent but slowly working its way through a recalcitrant material. This is a more plausible conception than that of a God who, though omnipotent and loving, has deliberately produced beings so subject to suffering and cruelty as the majority of mankind. I do not pretend to know that there is no such Purpose; my knowledge of the universe is too limited. But I do say, and I say with confidence, that the knowledge of other human beings is also limited, and that no one can adduce any good evidence that cosmic processes have any purpose whatever. Our very inadequate evidence, so far as it goes, tends in the opposite direction. . . .

Immortality, if we could believe in it, would enable us to shake off this gloom about the physical world. We should say that although our souls, during their sojourn here on earth, are in bondage to matter and physical laws, they pass at death into an eternal world beyond the empire of decay which science seems to reveal in the sensible world. But it is impossible to believe this unless we think that a human being consists of two parts—soul and body—which are separable and can continue independently of each other. Unfortunately all the evidence is against this. The mind grows like the body; like the body it inherits characteristics from both parents; it is affected by diseases of the body and by drugs; it is intimately connected with the brain. There is no scientific reason to suppose that after death the mind or soul acquires an independence of the brain which it never had in life. I do not pretend that this argument is conclusive, but it is all that we have to go upon except the slender evidence supplied by psychical research.

Many people fear that, without the theoretical beliefs that I find myself compelled to reject, the ethical beliefs which I accept could not survive. They point to the growth of cruel systems opposed to Christianity. But these systems, which grew up in a Christian atmosphere, could never have grown up if either kindly feeling or veracity had been practised; they are evil myths, inspired by hate and without scientific support. . . . The reasons for the ethic that, in common with many whose beliefs are more orthodox, I wish to see prevail are reasons derived from the course of events in this world. We have seen a great system of cruel falsehood, the Nazi system, lead a nation to disaster at immense cost to its opponents. It is not by such systems that happiness is to be achieved; even without the help of revelation it is not difficult to see that human welfare requires a less ferocious ethic. More and more people are becoming unable to accept traditional beliefs. If they think that, apart from these beliefs, there is no reason for kindly behaviour the results may be needlessly unfortunate. That is why it is important to show that no supernatural reasons are needed to make men kind and to prove that only through kindness can the human race achieve happiness.

'The Faith of a Rationalist' (Talk broadcast in 1947)

GEORGE EDWARD MOORE
1873–1958

Can 'Good' Be Defined?

What, then, is good? How is good to be defined? . . . My answer may seem a very disappointing one. If I am asked 'What is good?' my answer is that good is good, and that is the end of the matter. Or if I am asked 'How is good to be defined?' my answer is that it cannot be defined, and that is all I have to say about it. But disappointing as these answers may appear, they are of the very last importance. To readers who are familiar with philosophic terminology, I can express their importance by saying that they amount to this: That propositions about the good are all of them synthetic and never analytic; and that is plainly no trivial matter. And the same thing may be expressed more popularly, by saying that, if I am right, then nobody can foist upon us such an axiom as that 'Pleasure is the only good' or that 'The good is the desired' on the pretence that this is 'the very meaning of the word'.

Let us then, consider this position. My point is that 'good' is a simple notion, just as 'yellow' is a simple notion; that, just as you cannot, by any manner of means, explain to any one who does not already know it, what yellow is, so you cannot explain what good is. . . . 'Good' has no definition because it is simple and has no parts. It is one of those innumerable objects of thought which are themselves incapable of definition, because they are the ultimate terms by reference to which whatever is capable of definition must be defined. That there must be an indefinite number of such terms is obvious, on reflection; since we cannot define anything except by an analysis, which, when carried as far as it will go, refers us to something, which is simply different from anything else, and which by that ultimate difference explains the peculiarity of the whole which we are defining: for every whole contains some parts which are common to other wholes also. There is, therefore, no intrinsic difficulty in the contention that 'good' denotes a simple and indefinable quality. There are many other instances of such qualities.

Consider yellow, for example. We may try to define it, by describing its physical equivalent; we may state what kind of light-vibrations must stimulate the normal eye, in order that we may perceive it. But a moment's reflection is sufficient to show that those light-vibrations are not themselves what we mean by yellow. They are not what we perceive. Indeed we should never have been able to discover their existence, unless we had first been struck by the patent differences of quality between the different colours. The most we can be entitled to say of those vibrations is that they are what corresponds in space to the yellow which we actually perceive.

Yet a mistake of this simple kind has commonly been made about 'good'. it may be true that all things which are good are also something else (e.g. pleasant), just as it is true that all things which are yellow produce a certain kind of vibration in the light. And it is a fact, that Ethics aims at discovering what are those other properties belonging to all things which are good. But far too many philosophers have thought that when they named those other properties they were actually defining good; that these properties, in fact, were simply not 'other', but absolutely and entirely the same with goodness. This view I propose to call the 'naturalistic fallacy' and of it I shall not endeavour to dispose. . . .

Principia Ethica (1903), Chap. 1, 6, 10

Good as Means and Good as End

Our first conclusion as to the subject-matter of Ethics is, then, that there is a simple, indefinable, unanalysable object of thought by reference to which it must be defined. . . . All judgments (of the form 'so-and-so is good') refer to that unique notion . . . (but) they do not all refer to it in the same way. They may either assert that this unique property does always attach to the thing in question, or else they may assert only that the thing in question is a cause or necessary condition for the existence of other things to which this unique property does attach. The nature of these two species of universal ethical judgment is extremely different; and a great part of the difficulties, which are met with in ordinary ethical speculation, are due to the failure to distinguish them clearly. Their difference has, indeed, received expression in ordinary language by the contrast between the terms 'good as means' and 'good in itself', 'value as a means' and 'intrinsic value'. But these terms are apt to be applied correctly only in the more obvious instances; and this seems to be due to the fact that the distinction between the conceptions which they denote has not been made a separate object of investigation.

Ibid., 15

What Things Are Good as Ends?

The method which must be employed in order to decide the question 'What things have intrinsic value, and in what degrees?' has already been explained. . . . In order to arrive at a correct decision on the first part of this question, it is necessary to consider what things are such that, if they existed by themselves, in absolute isolation, we should yet judge their existence to be good; and, in order to decide upon the relative degrees of value of different things, we must similarly consider what comparative value seems to attach to the isolated existence of each.

If, now, we use this method of absolute isolation . . . it appears that the question we have to answer is far less difficult than the controversies of Ethics might have led us to expect. Indeed, once the meaning of the question is clearly understood, the answer to it, in its main outlines, appears to be so obvious, that it runs the risk of seeming to be a platitude. By far the most valuable things, which we know or can imagine, are certain states of consciousness, which may be roughly described as the pleasures of human intercourse and the enjoyment of beautiful objects. No one, probably, who has asked himself the question, has ever doubted that personal affection and the appreciation of what is beautiful in Art or Nature, are good in themselves; nor, if we consider strictly what things are worth having purely for their own sakes, does it appear probable that any one will think that anything else has nearly so great a value as the things which are included under these two heads. I have myself urged . . . that the mere existence of what is beautiful does appear to have some intrinsic value; but I regard it as indubitable that Prof. Sidgwick was so far right, in the view there discussed, that such mere existence of what is beautiful has value, so small as to be negligible, in comparison with that which attaches to the consciousness of beauty. This simple truth may, indeed, be said to be universally recognized. What has not been recognized is that it is the ultimate and fundamental truth of Moral Philosophy. That it is only for the sake of these things—in order that as much of them as possible may at some time exist—that any one can be justified in performing any public or private duty; that they are the *raison d'être* of virtue; that it is they—these complex wholes themselves, and not any constituent or characteristic of them—that form the rational ultimate end of human action and the sole criterion of social progress: these appear to be truths which have been generally overlooked.

Ibid., Chap. VI, 112, 113

ALBERT EINSTEIN
1879–1955

'A Deeply Religious Man'

The fairest thing we can experience is the mysterious. It is the fundamental emotion which stands at the cradle of true art and true science. He who knows it not and can no longer wonder, no longer feel amazement, is as good as dead, a snuffed-out candle. It was the experience of mystery—even if mixed with fear—that engendered religion. A knowledge of the existence of something we cannot penetrate, of the manifestations of the profoundest reason and the most radiant beauty, which are only accessible to our reason in their most elementary forms—it is this knowledge and this emotion that constitute the truly religious attitude; in this sense, and in this alone, I am a deeply religious man. I cannot conceive of a God who rewards and punishes his creatures, or has a will of the type of which we are conscious in ourselves. An individual who should survive his physical death is also beyond my comprehension, nor do I wish it otherwise; such notions are for the fears or absurd egoism of feeble souls. Enough for me the mystery of the eternity of life, and the inkling of the marvellous structure of reality, together with the single-hearted endeavour to comprehend a portion, be it ever so tiny, of the reason that manifests itself in nature.

The World as I See It (1934), Part I, trans. Alan Harris

The Meaning of 'Religious'

Instead of asking what religion is I should prefer to ask what characterizes the aspirations of a person who gives me the impression of being religious: A person who is religiously enlightened appears to me to be one who has, to the best of his ability, liberated himself from the fetters of his selfish desires and is preoccupied with thoughts, feelings, and aspirations to which he clings because of their super-personal value. It seems to me that what is important is the force of this super-personal content and the depth of the conviction concerning its overpowering meaningfulness, regardless of whether any attempt is made to unite this content with a divine Being, for otherwise it would not be possible to count Buddha and Spinoza as religious personalities.

'Science and Religion' (1941), reprinted in
Out of My Later Years (1950)

Science and Ethics

For the scientist, there is only 'being', but no wishing, no valuing, no good, no evil; no goal. As long as we remain within the realm of science proper, we can never meet with a sentence of the type: 'Thou shalt not lie'. There is something like a Puritan's restraint in the scientist who seeks truth: he keeps away from everything voluntaristic or emotional. Incidentally, this trait is the result of a slow development, peculiar to modern Western thought.

From this it might seem as if logical thinking were irrelevant for ethics. Scientific statements of facts and relations, indeed, cannot produce ethical directives. However, ethical directives can be made rational and coherent by logical thinking and empirical knowledge. If we can agree on some fundamental ethical propositions, then other ethical propositions can be derived from them, provided that the original premises are stated with sufficient precision. Such ethical premises play a similar role in ethics, to that played by axioms in mathematics.

This is why we do not feel at all that it is meaningless to ask such questions as: 'Why should we not lie?' We feel that such questions are meaningful because in all discussions of this kind some ethical premises are tacitly taken for granted. We then feel satisfied when we succeed in tracing back the ethical directive in question to these basic premises. In the case of lying this might perhaps be done in some way such as this: Lying destroys confidence in the statements of other people. Without such confidence, social cooperation is made impossible or at least difficult. Such cooperation, however, is essential to make human life possible and tolerable. This means that the rule 'Thou shalt not lie' has been traced back to the demands: 'Human life shall be preserved' and 'Pain and sorrow shall be lessened as much as possible.'

But what is the origin of such ethical axioms? Are they arbitrary? Are they based on mere authority? Do they stem from experiences of men and are they conditioned indirectly by such experiences?

For pure logic all axioms are arbitrary, including the axioms of ethics. But they are by no means arbitrary from a psychological and genetic point of view. They are derived from our inborn tendencies to avoid pain and annihilation, and from the accumulated emotional reaction of individuals to the behaviour of their neighbours.

It is the privilege of man's moral genius, impersonated by inspired individuals, to advance ethical axioms which are so comprehensive and so well founded that men will accept them as grounded in the vast mass of their individual emotional experiences. Ethical axioms are found and tested not very differently from the axioms of science. Truth is what stands the test of experience.

'The Laws of Science and the Laws of Ethics' (Preface to
Philipp, *Frank Relativity. A Richer Truth,* 1950,
reprinted in *Out of my Later Years,* 1950)

EDWARD MORGAN FORSTER (E. M. FORSTER)
1879–1970

Humanism versus Authoritarianism

Humanism covers my main belief and my main disbelief. My belief in the individual, and in his duty to create, and to understand and to contact other individuals. A duty that may be and ought to be a delight. The human race, to which he belongs, may not survive, but that should not deter him, nor should he be deterred by minatory theories about its origin nor by recent evidence that he, the individual, may be after all dividable. Wherever our race comes from, wherever it is going to, whatever his own fissures and weaknesses, he himself is here, is now, he must understand, create, contact. And this leads me to my main disbelief. I disbelieve in spiritual authority, however sincerely exercised and however nobly garbed. It is right to be respectful to other individuals and indeed to certain institutions, and to listen to what they have to say: one knows little enough and must seize every opportunity. But to believe anything because someone has said it or because some institution has promulgated it seems to be dead wrong. Many people—people of ability, insight and virtue—will say that it is I who am wrong here. If they say that, they are not humanists. I am a humanist. Here is the dividing line.

My attitude towards religion may seem to such people very foolish. I like, or anyhow tolerate, most religions so long as they are weak, and I find in their rites an acknowledgment of our smallness which is salutary. But I dread them all, without exception, as soon as they become powerful. All power corrupts. Absolute power which believes itself the instrument of absolute truth corrupts absolutely. Why shouldn't it? Why should not Certainty dictate? To take some examples; nothing could be more sensitive, cultivated and understanding than Roman Catholicism in an English University, where it must expect competition. Roman Catholicism in Ireland, where it is strong and unchecked, is a very different matter. . . . Another example: the protean movement which has been successively known as Buchmanism, the Oxford Group, and Moral Rearmament. It is understandable that the founder of this movement should have once exclaimed: 'Thank God for Hitler.' It is to be hoped he will find no dictator to succeed Hitler. (Another) example: the religious aspect of Marxism, which tolerates no rival, once it is established. 'Catholicism is the only alternative to Communism', a slogan often heard here, is probably echoed on the other side of the Iron Curtain.

I assert that there is an alternative in humanism.

In the present rise of obscurantism amongst intellectuals, humanism is seldom directly attacked. Perhaps they do not consider it sufficiently important. 'Elbowed out' would be the better

phrase. Its stronghold in history, the Renaissance, is alleged not
to have existed. Its conception of human nature, and its hopes for
it are implicitly denied by emphasizing the arbitrary theory of
Original Sin. It is regarded, at most, as a weakness in the wall of
western defence through which a rival ideology might percolate.
I have found it something more positive than this, something life-
giving, something which has made the world of the past fifty
years exciting and valuable and sometimes comprehensible, and
I am very glad, sir, that The Twentieth Century should be opening its columns to honour it. The celebration won't, I hope, take
too much the form of a Campaign. Campaigns tend to assimilate
the rival campaigners. Humanism could better be honoured by
reciting a list of the things one has enjoyed or found interesting,
of the people who have helped one, and of the people whom one
has loved and tried to help. The list would not be dramatic, it
would lack the sonority of a creed and the solemnity of a sanction,
but it could be recited confidently, for human gratitude and human
hopefulness would be speaking.

Letter to *The Twentieth Century,* 1955

Humanist Belief

I do not believe in Belief. But this is an Age of Faith, and there are
so many militant creeds that, in self-defence, one has to formu-
late a creed of one's own. Tolerance, good temper and sympathy
are no longer enough in a world which is rent by religious and
racial persecution, in a world where ignorance rules, and Science,
who ought to have ruled, plays the subservient pimp. Tolerance,
good temper and sympathy—they are what matter really, and if
the human race is not to collapse they must come to the front
before long. But for the moment they are not enough, their action
is no stronger than a flower, battered beneath a military jack-
boot. They want stiffening, even if the process coarsens them.
Faith, to my mind, is a stiffening process, a sort of mental starch,
which ought to be applied as sparingly as possible. I dislike the
stuff. I do not believe in it, for its own sake, at all. Herein I probably differ from most people, who believe in Belief, and are only
sorry they cannot swallow even more than they do. My law-givers
are Erasmus and Montaigne, not Moses and St. Paul. My temple

stands not upon Mount Moriah but in that Elysian Field where even the immoral are admitted. My motto is: 'Lord, I disbelieve—help thou my unbelief.'

What I Believe (1939)

HENRY LOUIS MENCKEN
1880–1956

'Interimsethik'

The chief peculiarities of the Christian moral system, as it is distinguished from the Jewish and Greek systems on which it is mainly based, issue from an error in fact made by Jesus, and not abandoned by his followers until it was too late to rectify its consequences. That was the error of supposing the end of the world to be at hand. It is common today for Christian theologians to deny that Jesus believed this, but the texts in point are too explicit to be argued away. They report a conversation with the disciples in the vicinity of Caesarea Philippa, and appear in all three of the Synoptic Gospels. . . .'There be some standing here which shall not taste of death, till they see the Son of Man coming in his kingdom' (Matthew xvi, 28). In Luke ix, 27, the last clause is changed to 'till they see the kingdom of God' and in Mark ix, 1, to 'till they have seen the kingdom of God come with power', but these variations are plainly immaterial. In Mark xii, 30, there is the additional assurance that 'this generation shall not pass till all these things be done'. . . . In Mark xiii, 32, the disciples are informed, apparently in response to their natural inquiries, that the precise day and hour 'knoweth no man, no, not the angels which are in heaven, neither the Son, but the Father', and there are other cautions to the same purport elsewhere, but always it is made plain that the time will be in the near future, and in Matthew x the disciples are sent forth to preach with the assurance that it 'is at hand'. . . .

The denunciation, trial and execution of Jesus seems to have shaken the disciples' faith in his divine mission, and with it their belief in the cardinal articles of his prophecy. . . . But as news of the resurrection spread up and down the Eastern Mediterranean coast, and the first Christian revival got under way, all such doubts were engulfed in a wave of enthusiasm amounting almost to frenzy, and the disciples, like the rank and file, were ready to believe anything. On the Day of Pentecost, as we learn from Acts ii, they heard a mighty wind roar down from the heavens, saw 'cloven tongues as of fire', and began to jabber gibberish in the manner of converts at a Holy Roller camp-meeting. Their preaching to the throngs that crowded about them was thoroughly millennial. They taught that 'the last days were at hand', that the appropriate signs and portents were already visible, and that it behoved every prudent man to get rid of his 'possessions and goods' and prepare for the reappearance of Jesus, 'sitting on the right hand of power and coming in the clouds of heaven' to work the Last Judgment.

Out of all this flowed what the German higher critics call the *Interimsethik,* which is to say, a scheme of stop-gap ethics for the brief interval between an unhappy and hopeless today and a glorious and near tomorrow. It rejected many of the values that mankind had cherished immemorially. Industry, thrift, justice, temperance, and fidelity to family and fatherland were swept away as vain and useless in the premises, and the new morality counselled instead the giving away of all worldly goods, the abandonment of wife and child, the renunciation of racial and national pride, and the intensive practice of such humble virtues as might be expected to flatter a regal and exacting Yahweh—meekness, self-abasement, patience under injustice, complete chastity, and so on—above all, a simple and grovelling faith. To a large extent this programme was based on the reported sayings of Jesus, for example in the Beatitudes, in the denunciation of riches in Mark x, 25 (which so astonished the disciples), in Matthew vi, 34 ('Take therefore no thought for the morrow'), and in the various categorical prophecies of the early end of the world, already quoted. But there were extensive ratifications by the disciples in the first days of the infant Church, and many more followed when Paul began his mission. In Thessalonians i he assures his correspondents that 'we which are alive and remain shall be caught up together with them in the clouds, to meet the Lord in the air'; in I Corinthians vii and x he gives them warning that 'the time is short' and 'the ends of the world are come'; and in Philippians iv, 5, he says flatly that 'the Lord is at hand'. . . .

As time passed and (the Judgment) failed to come off there

must have been a good deal of murmuring among the faithful, for some of the rigours ordained in preparation for it were not a little onerous. . . . Their demands for the exact date of their release from these rigours had to be met, and meeting them was not easy. Paul, in his Second Epistle to the Thessalonians, tried to get rid of the question by answering that a great many marvels would have to happen first, including the coming of Antichrist. In this he was supported, though he did not mention it, by Jesus's own prophecy in Mark xiii: 'nation shall rise against nation, and kingdom against kingdom: and there shall be earthquakes in divers places, and there shall be famines and troubles.' But there must have been many among the faithful who believed that enough woes were already upon the world to justify the immediate commencement of the final catastrophe, and these seem to have been rather pressing in their inquiries. In II Peter iii, 8, Simon Peter is recorded as seeking to put them off by arguing somewhat lamely that 'one day is with the Lord as a thousand years'—an argument that was to be revived nearly two thousand years later by those doomed by an unhappy fate to attempt to reconcile the facts of geology with the cosmogony of Genesis.

It took a long while for hopes in the Second Coming to die out. There was in them so much consolation for poor and miserable men, and they were so thoroughly in accord with the apocalyptic prepossessions of the time, that they survived long after it must have been evident to every rational person that Jesus and Paul had been mistaken. Down through the first century there were frequent reports that the great day was at hand, and after the fall of Jerusalem in the year 70 it was looked for with new confidence. In the latter part of the second century there was a great revival of hopes led by one Montanus, a convert to Christianity from the cult of Cybele, the Great Mother, whom he had served as a priest in Phrygia. . . . (But) the great battle over the nature and attributes of the Trinity, which began toward the close of the second century, became so violent during the next hundred years that the theologians of the young Church had little time left to debate the Second Coming, and without doubt most of them were glad to be rid of it. Thus the *Interimsethik* lost much of its force, and the majority of the faithful, led by their pastors, began to show an interest in worldly values.

Treatise on Right and Wrong (1934), Chap. IV, 2, 3

SIR JULIAN HUXLEY
1887–1975

A Humanist's Faith

I use the word humanist to mean someone who believes that man is just as much a natural phenomenon as an animal or a plant, that his body, his mind, and his soul were not supernaturally created but are all products of evolution, and that he is not under the control or guidance of any supernatural Being or beings, but has to rely on himself and his own powers. And I use faith in the sense of a set of essentially religious beliefs.

How then can a humanist be religious? Is not religion necessarily concerned with supernatural beings? The answer is 'No.' Religion of some sort seems always to have been a feature of man's life; but some religions are not concerned with God, and some not with any sort of supernatural beings at all. Religions are of many kinds, good and bad, primitive and advanced: but they all have one thing in common—they help man to cope with the problem of his place and role in the strange universe in which he lives.

Religion . . . always involves the sense of sacredness or reverence, and it is always concerned with what is felt to be more absolute, with what transcends immediate, particular, everyday experience. It aims at helping people to transcend their petty or selfish or guilty selves. All organized religions not only have a set of rituals but a moral code—what is right and what is wrong: and a system of beliefs. In the long run, the beliefs determine the moral code, and they in their turn are based on man's knowledge of himself and the world.

Humanist beliefs are based on human knowledge, especially on the knowledge-explosion of the hundred years since Darwin published *The Origin of Species,* which has revealed to us a wholly new picture of the universe and of our place in it. We now believe with confidence that the whole of reality is one gigantic process of evolution. This produces increased novelty and variety, and ever higher types of organization; in a few spots it has produced life; and, in a few of those spots of life, it has produced mind and consciousness.

This universal process is divisible into three phases or sectors, each with its own method of working, its own rate of change, and its own kind of results. Over most of the universe it is in the lifeless or inorganic phase. On earth (and undoubtedly on some planets of other suns) it is in the organic or biological phase. This works by natural selection and has produced a huge variety of animals and plants, some astonishingly high organizations (like our own bodies, or an ant colony), and the emergence of mind.

Finally man (and possibly a few other organisms elsewhere) has entered the human or, as we may call it, psychosocial phase, which is based on the accumulation of knowledge and the organization of experience. It works chiefly by a conscious selection of ideas and aims, and produces extremely rapid change. Evolution in this phase is mainly cultural, not genetic; it is no longer focused solely on survival, but is increasingly directed towards fulfilment and towards quality of achievement.

Man is the latest dominant type of life on this earth, and the sole agent for its further evolution. He is the product of more than two and a half million years of past evolution; and we believe that he has at least an equally vast span of future evolution before him.

Though human evolution has been accompanied by much evil and horror it has led to real advance (for instance, in health and length of life), and has produced great new achievements (such as cathedrals and aeroplanes, poems and philosophies, arts and sciences). And this has been due to the increase of human experience and knowledge and its better organization in concepts and scientific laws, in ideas and works of art. We know that a large number of things that used to be supposed to be due to supernatural intervention are nothing of the sort, but are the result of perfectly natural causes. We do not believe that epidemics are divine punishments, or earthquakes divine warnings; we do not believe that witches are in league with the Devil, or that artistic inspiration comes from a supernatural source; prayers for rain are still offered in church, but very few people (and no humanists) believe that God has any influence on the weather. We know that there is no hell full of devils inside the earth, and nothing like the traditional orthodox Christian idea of heaven up in the sky.

But we have faith in the capacities and possibilities of man: most immediately in his capacity to accumulate his experience, and in the resultant possibilities of increasing his knowledge and understanding. We have seen their results in science and medicine; we have faith in their possibilities for psychology and politics, for conservation and eugenics. But we must think of man's other capacities, too. His capacity for disinterested curiosity and wonder leads him both to seek and to enjoy knowledge. His capacity for enjoying beauty pushes him to create, to preserve, and to contemplate it. His capacity to feel guilt impels him towards morality, his sense of incompleteness leads him to seek greater wholeness. He is endowed with a sense of justice which slowly but steadily brings about the remedying of injustice. He has a capacity for compassion which leads him to care for the sick, the aged, and the persecuted, and a capacity for love which could (and sometimes does) override his capacity for hate.

Many human possibilities are still unrealized save by a few: the possibility of enjoying experiences of transcendent rapture, physical and mystical, aesthetic and religious, or that of attaining an inner harmony and peace that puts a man above the cares and worries of daily life. Indeed man as a species has not yet realized more than a fraction of his possibilities of health, physical and mental, and spiritual well-being, of achievement and knowledge, of wisdom and enjoyment, or of satisfaction in participating in worth-while or enduring projects, including that most enduring of all projects, man's further evolution.

So man's most sacred duty is to realize his possibilities of knowing, feeling, and willing to the fullest extent, in the development of human individuals, in the achievements of human societies, and in the evolution of the whole human species. I believe that an understanding of the extent to which man falls short of realizing his splendid possibilities will stimulate him to learn how they can be realized, and that this will be the most powerful religious motive in the next stage of our human evolution. As a humanist, that is my faith.

'The Faith of a Humanist' (Talk broadcast in 1960)

M. N. ROY
1887–1954

Radical Democracy

Democracy can be established only by the reassertion of the humanist tradition. Man is the measure of his world. Being inherently rational, he can always learn from experience. He develops his intellectual faculties and moral values in his effects to secure a better life for himself. That ability is not confined to a few, nor acquired at a particular economic level. While economic sufficiency may be helpful to cultural growth, the view that the one is the precondition of the other is historically false and logically untenable. Man's faculties have developed in the course of his struggle for existence.

Throughout the course of history, spiritual revolts have always preceded great social changes. Mental freedom has necessarily been the precondition for any attempt to attain political and economic freedom. Faced with economic insufficiency, political oppression and social instability, the people can nevertheless develop the will as well as the ability to change that situation. Scientific humanism precludes the view that the will to freedom and the ability to attain it are accessible only to a minority, which is thus qualified for leadership.

A survey of the main features of the contemporary crisis reinforces the conclusion already reached by Radical Democrats, that a political party striving for power cannot be the means to the attainment of freedom. A movement for freedom as visualised in the philosophy of New Humanism must be broader than a political movement, nor can it be organised and led by a political party of the traditional type. Standing outside the scramble for power, it will seek to educate people in the cultural values essential for the realisation of democracy. Creation of a new outlook of life will be its primary function and, in the conditions prevailing in India, its major preoccupation for some length of time. On that basis, it will develop democratic institutions which will bring about the widest diffusion of power. The impact of its ideas will not be limited to political and economic spheres. It will result in the rise of new men and women engaged in the task of establishing new forms of social relations and building new patterns of political institutions. The movement will be a comprehensive, intellectual, social movement.

from *Practice of New Humanism* (1953)

The Spirit of Enquiry

Thus we come to the fundamental task that confronts the young intellectuals of our country today. The task is not to revive religion, but to subject religion to a dispassionate criticism. We have heard some of the modern religionists declare that the idea of God must be rejected, if it cannot stand the test of reason. You apply that test to religion, and all that which goes under the pompous denomination of our spiritual culture, and the whole structure of religion will collapse like a house of cards. Only it is not as easily collapsible as a house of cards. It still stands with apparent solidity, but on a decayed foundation. Dig into the foundation and the whole decayed structure will crash.

I appeal to you to be rational, critical, inspired with the spirit of enquiry. Don't take things simply for granted. If you do not have the courage to revolt against authority outright, then at least go to the extent of demanding on what sanction is the authority based. You shall never be able to be free on this earth so long as you remain a voluntary subject to forces unknown and unknowable. Only men who are spiritually free can lead an entire nation in a great revolutionary movement. Intellectuals must be free in spirit. Only as such can they take their proud position in society. Let us get rid of pseudo-intellectualism which tries to rationalise the irrational. Remember that even the great die. Whatever may have been the greatness of our past it is dead. You cannot revive it. The prisoners of the past can never be the masters of the future.

Ibid.

BARBARA FRANCES WOOTTON (Baroness Wootton)
1897–1988

Faith and Science

The whole attitude to doubt is, indeed, a critical test of the difference between faith and scientific knowledge. The believer must not keep an open mind, ready to abandon his faith should the weight of evidence seem to point that way. To the faithful doubt is a sin: to the scientist it is the first of all virtues. To appreciate the width of the gulf between them, one only has to match the spectacle of the Christian 'fighting hard for his belief' with a parallel image of the scientist wrestling with his soul in the laboratory in a struggle to remain unconvinced by the evidence of nuclear fission. It may be true that men of science acquire a vested interest in their own theories, so that they may be reluctant, for instance, to see the work of a lifetime superseded by later discoveries: hence Darwin's practice of noting with special care evidence which ran counter to his theories. But, as Darwin's example shows, to resist doubt is the scientist's temptation—the believer's triumph.

Testament for Social Science (1950), Chap. V, 2

Religion and the Social Sciences

It is certainly true that science and religion do not now fight over the same ground as they did even as recently as the nineteenth century; but it does not, I think, follow that the battle is over, at least so far as the social sciences are concerned. . . . If the natural sciences are no longer in conflict with religion, it is because religion no longer dares to say anything about the behaviour of natural phenomena, having always been proved wrong when it did so. . . .

Religion could (however) retreat, without catastrophic loss, before the advance of the natural sciences, since this did not disturb its occupation of the whole field of human experience and relations. But the advance of science, and particularly of the social sciences, into this territory contains a new and still more alarming threat; because if this province is lost, there will be precious little left at all. Since the social sciences are only in their infancy, the threat is only just beginning to take shape; but there is little doubt that as it develops with the progress of these sciences, there will again be fierce battles, of which only the first skirmishes have yet been seen. The physical and human sciences between them have already begun to establish laws of association between physical events in the brain and mental experiences: there is at least a risk that in time they will find that the religious experiences now accepted as communion with God may also be associated with purely human events, mental or physical, and explicable therefore on an entirely godless hypothesis. Further, brain surgery can already profoundly modify personality and patterns of behaviour; and psychiatry has begun to account for moral conviction in terms which make any deity superfluous. . . .

It is, of course, possible (for religion) to retreat again: to argue that just as God controls the behaviour of atoms and of physical objects indirectly through the laws of physics, or the state of our health indirectly through the laws of physiology and chemistry, instead of by direct personal manipulation, so also he controls our mental processes no less indirectly through the laws of physiology and psychology, including those that govern the operations of the unconscious mind. . . . The dangers of this road of escape should, however, be obvious. For a God who leaves not only physical occurrences, but also mental and spiritual and moral experiences, to the mercy of impersonal and unchanging laws of association becomes extraordinarily remote and unsatisfying. It would be difficult to keep up friendship, much more to feel passionate devotion, towards anyone whose sole response on all occasions was: 'I am sorry, but I cannot do anything about it: the matter is now outside my control.' It must be hardly less difficult to worship or to love a God, who, having invented the laws of psychology and physiology, leaves suffering humanity to make the best of the consequences. Indeed, as first physical, then mental, emotional and even spiritual events become more and more clearly governed by laws of association between empirical phenomena, and therefore less and less occasion for the direct intervention of the deity, we get nearer and nearer to the point at which the difference between a religious and a secular interpretation of the universe becomes negligible. . . .

Nevertheless, up till now a number of professional students of the social sciences have retained a religious and sometimes even a specifically Christian faith. They have had to throw away a lot of bath water, but have succeeded in persuading themselves that at least some sort of a baby has, by various compromises, been retained. No compromise, however, can conceal the fundamental dilemma that the more specific the faith or doctrine, the more vulnerable it is to the advance of science; or that, conversely, surrender on specific points leads by an inevitable gradualness to the dissolution of anything that is worth calling a religion at all. Certainly, in my experience, many students who have been brought up in a Christian or other specifically religious faith, and who turn to the study of the social sciences, reach a point at which they are troubled by the difficulty of reconciling their religion and their scientific studies. Sometimes at this stage they give up their sociological inquiries, unable to 'follow the argument whithersoever it leads': sometimes they accept one or other of the current compromises, throwing away as much of the specific content of their religion as they dare; and sometimes their religious faith surrenders completely to the relentless encroachments of science. But whatever the outcome, the conflict that they glimpse at the moment of crisis is profoundly real. Whatever subsequent adjustment each may personally make, the incompatibility of the uninhibited pursuit of science and of faith in (a personal God) remains. Meantime deep and unnecessary misery is inflicted on all who, because they have been taught from childhood to accept as sacred fact what is merely somebody's guess, grow up afraid to discard their religious swaddling clothes.

Ibid., Chap. V, 3

GORA (FOUNDER OF ATHEIST CENTRE, INDIA)
1902–1975

The Atheistic Way of Life

The essence of atheism is the freedom of the individual. Freedom releases the immense potentialities of human imagination, initiative and effort that lay suppressed under theistic faith. Free individuals feel masters of situations. The mood of supplication and complaint, inherent in prayer to god and petitions to government, has no place in the atheistic way of life. Atheists always assert; they never surrender. They take no failure; everything is an experience that improves the method for further attempts.

Atheists too have their faiths, fancies and ideals. But their scientific outlook distinguishes between faith and truth. Accordingly the purpose of life changes. It is not the fanciful salvation after death, but happiness here and now. So, with technological skill, atheists harness wind, water and earth for the fulfilment of man's desires. They endeavour to control drought and disease and bid fair to conquer death. The by-products of artificialness, like overpopulation, pollution and depletion of natural resources, are dealt with realistically through decentralization.

Atheists face facts without fear. 'What is to be done?' concerns them more than 'Why is it so?' Findings of postmortems in social affairs have their limitations with atheists who open new avenues with fresh initiative every time. For history seldom repeats itself with atheists.

The mundaneness of atheists does not stagnate in self-indulgence. Kings and capitalists had to escape into spirituality for peace and consolation. Atheistic mundaneness, on the contrary, increases social awareness and keeps atheists busy in zealously guarding the needs of honesty and equality. Atheists are militantly social. Injustice and inequality anywhere is the active concern of everyone everywhere. Obviously, poverty, violence and discrimination have no place among atheists.

The distinction between the majority and the minority communities loses validity in the atheistic way of life. Whatever label minorities take, race, language, nationality, culture, economic opportunity or political party, all claims of minorities are basically sectarian. Atheism which mingles all people alike in one humanity cannot allow such claims. Everyone has to feel free and live equal with another, without taking shelter under the cover of a label.

Positive Atheism (1972)

SIDNEY HOOK
1902–1989

The Snare of Definitions

The logic of definitions is quite complex. Unless we are clear about the point and purpose of a definition, its context in use and inquiry, it may create more difficulties than it solves.

This is particularly true with respect to the definition of humanism. One danger lies in defining humanism so broadly that it includes many who have defended monstrous crimes against human freedom; who have, for instance, been professional apologists of Stalin's terroristic regime, including the infamous Moscow Purge Trials and other practices exposed by Khruschev in his Report to the Twentieth Congress of the CPSU. Some definitions of humanism are so broad that they would embrace defenders of the regimes of Salazar and Franco, who also profess a belief in 'the brotherhood of man'. Such definitions of humanism are as worthless as definitions of 'democracy' (very fashionable these days) that include perfervid partisans of minority party dictatorships.

The converse difficulty is defining humanism too narrowly. We then exclude individuals with whom we feel a strong moral kinship and who, despite some metaphysical or even theological overbeliefs that seem to have no perceptible bearing on their conduct, are comrades, or at least co-belligerents, in every good cause. Any definition that excludes them seems inadequate. . . .

Definitions of humanism should avoid the pitfall of so defining it that it excludes no one. If the Holy Grail is everywhere there is no point in its quest! For example, in an otherwise historically scholarly article in the *Encyclopaedia of Philosophy* we are told that: humanism is also any philosophy which recognizes the value or dignity of man and makes him the measure of all things or somehow [*sic!*] takes human nature, its limits, or its interests as its theme: Surely this is too broad! It catches almost everyone in its far-flung net. Who denies the value of man? Not even the Torquemadas of this world. Since both Protagoras and Socrates are humanists, it is not necessary to make the view that man is the measure of all things a necessary element in the definition of humanism. It would exclude not only Socrates but atheistic humanists like Bertrand Russell and Morris R. Cohen to whom the Protagorean dictum was anathema. To them, the proposition that man is the measure of all things is an expression of self-defeating subjectivity.

As a first step towards clarification of issues and standpoints, I should like to propose that humanism today be regarded primarily as an ethical doctrine and movement. We already have a term in use, the connotations of which embrace what is generally meant by 'scientific humanist'—viz. 'naturalism'.

There are humanists who are naturalists John Dewey), humanists who are supernaturalists (like William James) and humanists who are non-naturalists (like Felix Adler and G. E. Moore). These men differ not in their chief ethical values but in their meta-ethical analysis of the meanings and justification of the 'good' and 'right'.

Religion, as a system of overbeliefs about the existence of God and related views, I regard as a *private* matter. So long as I am not requested to give it any public support or affirmation, I have no more desire to expose, refute or confound it than I do my neighbour's belief that his wife is the most beautiful woman in the world. (The 'truth' is, of course, that mine is!) I have grown weary of being told that my 'concern' with human freedom or the 'fire in my heart' that blazes up when I hear of human cruelty is evidence of my religious nature.

Abstractly, except when two terms are exhaustive and exclusive of the alternatives, it is absurd to define a term by its negations, for such definition does not distinguish it from other terms in an indeterminedly large universe of discourse. But in specific, historical contexts sometimes we can make progress towards an adequate definition when we stress what we want to exclude. I do not regard as humanists today any individuals or groups:

(1) who believe or support doctrines and practices that would impose one pattern of culture, language and life-style on all members or groups in the community;

(2) who believe in an established Church or Churches, or that they have been vouchsafed revelations about their special character, justifying privileges and rights denied to other human beings;

(3) who believe in or support through their own voluntary activities dictatorships of minority political parties no matter whether they are called 'organic', 'directed', 'higher' or 'socialist' democracies;

(4) who deny community responsibility for the elimination of human hunger and for the progressive realization of civilized standards of housing, health, welfare and education;

(5) who denigrate the use of intelligence, justify violence in human affairs as the most effective method of achieving social reform, substitute lynch law (white or black) for judicial process, oppose *opportunities* for racial integration;

(6) who place loyalty to any organization of which they are members above any or all of the above values, who cherish any truth, offered as a ground for public action, above the evidence on which it allegedly rests, who profess to be tolerant but who, out of stupidity or cowardice, tolerate those who are actively intolerant in social and, especially, intellectual life.

If I had to propose a short positive definition on the basis of these negations, I would say that an ethical humanist today is one who relies on the arts of intelligence to defend, enlarge and enhance the areas of human freedom in the world. Ethical humanists may differ from each other, but they respect those with whom they disagree. They are not fanatics of virtue. They recognize that good conflicts with good, right with right, and sometimes the good with the right. To these conflicts they bring the only value that is also the judge of its own efficacy and limitation—human intelligence.

The Humanist Alternative: Some Definitions of Humanism,
ed. by Paul Kurtz (1973)

HAROLD JOHN BLACKHAM
1903–

Balance

A human being, it has already been said, should try to maintain a temporal balance in his life, so that each phase of his development is lived and enjoyed for its own sake and at the same time draws on the past and prepares for the future. This is a main condition of identity, continuity and achievement. Another main form of balance is between independence and interdependence, personal interests and social responsibility. The rules for living and working together which express and regulate our interdependence are a necessary condition of independence in a modern society, and therefore the public spirit with which we observe them faithfully ourselves and require others to do the same is merely a recognition that all should be equally free to pursue their own interests. It is the spirit of good faith and fair-mindedness among equals, and it is whole-hearted and unreserved. Either it is there altogether or it is not there at all. Therefore there is no call here for a balance between independence and interdependence: the two are reciprocal. But apart from this public spirit that keeps the rules and sees that others also do so there may be voluntary social service in aid of those who need help, which draws on time and resources and does call for a balance, since it is more or less, not all or none.

This personal dependence one on another as distinct from political interdependence is not measurable and cannot be regulated by rules. Very, very many people suffer severe handicaps of birth or misfortune, not to speak of their own failures and follies, which ask to be relieved if they are not to be left to endure a lot of unspeakable hardness. Of course a Welfare State is an attempt to reduce this dependency to measure and to rule: I pay my rates and taxes, and am quit of this obligation. But the obligation cannot be altogether disposed of in this way, because the need is too extensive and too personal and because it exists also and in greater measure far beyond the frontiers of the Welfare State. The individual is left to say what he will do about it on his own. At the extremes, he is not prepared to do anything or he decides to live with and for others a life of total service. Neither extreme is a characteristic humanist choice. Total disregard of the immeasurable demands of human need is not characteristic because humanism is an acceptance of responsibility for the life of mankind and acknowledges a sense of human solidarity. Total service, which amounts to a total disregard of one's own interests, is not characteristic because the pursuit of a chosen excellence, the cultivation of enjoyment, the development of one's own response to the world, are ways in which one knows and affirms the final value of human life. To devote oneself solely to the supposed good of others is too likely to be an inauthentic life, an avoidance of the issue. Perhaps this is what is really meant by 'living on Christian capital'. For it is quite otherwise for the Christian who in the grace of God already enjoys the supreme and only good, and therefore can live wholly to seek the same good for others. The humanist must verify for himself the final value of human life in his own experience and purposes before he can have reasonable confidence that the human lot is worth redeeming.

Humanism (1968)

The Open Mind

Assumption—responsibility—response: these three natural roots of humanism involve the three sides of human nature usually spoken of as intellect, will and feeling. All three sides are equally important to humanists as to others. But the humanist is a rationalist, one who puts reason first; and he stresses the open mind, dedication to a disinterested search for truth. There seem to be contradictions here if humanism begins with two massive assumptions which close the mind and put a dogmatic end to the disinterested search for truth.

The cult of an open mind and talk of a disinterested quest for truth is usually cant, and invites a good spit. However, two things have to be said in justification of this way of speaking. The open mind is an empty mind if it never makes up its mind. This cannot be what is meant. Second, although it would be absurd to think of humanists as engaged night and day (or even on Tuesdays and Thursdays) in a disinterested pursuit of truth, care for truth as a primary value is a distinguishing characteristic of humanists. They want to know first on what ground they can dig dependable foundations and build their house. When they have taken considerable trouble to do this, they are like other people; they have a vested interest, and do not want to have to evacuate or demolish their home. However, they are not worse than others at seeing that this may be necessary and recognizing when it has become necessary. They ought to be much better at this than others, and perhaps most of them really are.

The faith of the humanist is first of all in reason, in the reliability of tested evidence. There are some matters in which the head is sovereign, some in which the heart is queen. When Pascal says, 'The heart has its reasons of which reason knows nothing', he is commending trust in the heart rather the head on some matters. There are matters of choice on which the heart is entitled to have the main say, but the choice of life is certainly not one of them—in the humanist's view. If the humanist did have a religious faith, he would hold it conditionally on rational grounds, retaining his primary faith in reason. In the days of natural religion, in the eighteenth century, this was done. With the subsequent erosion of the foundations of natural theology this position has collapsed. The three pillars of reason have become pillars of unreason. A resort to the reasons of the heart which the mind does not comprehend looks tricky. An open mind means a candour to which trickery is repugnant. It means exposure, not covering up the vulnerable places. An open mind is vulnerable to evidence.

Ibid.

MARGARET KENNEDY KNIGHT
1903–1983

Religion and Moral Training

In a climate of thought that is increasingly unfavourable to (Christian) beliefs, it is a mistake to try to impose them on children, and to make them the basis of moral training. The moral education of children is much too important a matter to be built on such foundations. . . .

If (a child) is brought up in the orthodox way, he will accept what he is told happily enough to begin with. But if he is normally intelligent, he is almost bound to get the impression that there is something odd about religious statements. If he is taken to church, for example, he hears that death is the gateway to eternal life, and should be welcomed rather than shunned; yet outside he sees death regarded as the greatest of all evils, and everything possible done to postpone it. In church he hears precepts like 'Resist not evil', and 'Take no thought for the morrow'; but he soon realizes that these are not really meant to be practised outside. If he asks questions, he gets embarrassed, evasive answers: 'Well, dear, you're not quite old enough to understand yet, but some of these things are true in a deeper sense'; and so on. The child soon gets the idea that there are two kinds of truth—the ordinary kind, and another, rather confusing and slightly embarrassing kind, into which it is best not to inquire too closely.

Now all this is bad intellectual training. It tends to produce a certain intellectual timidity—a distrust of reason—a feeling that it is perhaps rather bad taste to pursue an argument to its logical conclusion, or to refuse to accept a belief on inadequate evidence. And that is not a desirable attitude in the citizens of a free democracy. However, it is the moral rather than the intellectual dangers that I am concerned with here; and they arise when the trustful child becomes a critical adolescent. He may then cast off all his religious beliefs; and, if his moral training has been closely tied up with religion, it is more than possible that the moral beliefs will go too.

'Morals without Religion' (Talk broadcast in 1955, reprinted in *Morals without Religion,* 1955)

Morals without Religion

Why should I consider others? These ultimate moral questions, like all ultimate questions, can be desperately difficult to answer, as every philosophy student knows. Myself, I think the only possible answer to this question is the humanist one—because we are naturally social beings; we live in communities; and life in any community, from the family outwards, is much happier, and fuller, and richer if the members are friendly and co-operative than if they are hostile and resentful. But the religious listener may feel that this is simply evading the point. So may I say in conclusion that the answer he would propose is not really any more satisfactory? His answer to the question 'Why should I consider others;' is 'Because it is God's will'. But the sceptic could always answer: 'Why should I do God's will? Why shouldn't I please myself?'—and that, surely, is just as much of a poser as 'Why should I consider others?'

In fact, it is a good deal more of a poser, in view of some of the things that the believer must suppose God to have willed. But we need not go into all that again, for in any case this question of ultimate sanctions is largely theoretical. I have never yet met the child—and I have met very few adults—to whom it has ever occurred to raise the question 'Why should I consider others?' Most people are prepared to accept as a completely self-evident moral axiom that we must not be completely selfish, and if we base our moral training on that we shall, I suggest, be building on firm enough foundations.

Ibid., Chap. 2

The essence of humanism is that it is non-supernatural. It is concerned with man rather than God, and with this life rather than the next. Its morality derives from the altruistic impulses, reinforced by training, not from divine commands; the moral act, to the humanist, is the act that is conducive to human well-being, not the act ordained by God.

The implication of 'scientific' is that the humanist tries to be disinterested in the intellectual as well as the moral sphere. He has the scientist's attitude of respect for evidence and 'humility before the facts'; and he applies this attitude to human affairs as well as to nature. When he is confronted with a human problem, such as an increase in juvenile delinquency or industrial disputes, his first reaction is that of the scientist—'let's find out'. He does not merely become indignant, or exhort or denounce without knowing the facts. He does not express 'views' unsupported by evidence. He proceeds objectively to investigate the cause of the problem, as the preliminary to doing something constructive about it. He is as much concerned with morality as the Christian, but he believes that virtue is more effective when it is illuminated by knowledge.

In preparing the broadcasts, I tried also to destroy the stereotyped picture of the non-Christian. There are two main versions of this. One is 'the atheist'. He is envisaged as a strident, loud-voiced and wholly insensitive individual, who equates 'the good' with material goods, and is always, of course, a Communist. Then there is 'the unbeliever'. He is a gentler type, usually thought of as wistful, rootless and suffering from a 'deep sense of loss'. The many well-balanced, warmhearted, cheerful and sensitive humanists, that most of us know, are ignored. I tried to suggest their existence.

Ibid., Chap. 3, 'The Reaction'

JEAN PAUL SARTRE
1905–1980

Existentialism and Humanism

When we think of God as the creator, we are thinking of him, most of the time, as a supernal artisan. Whatever doctrine we may be considering, whether it be a doctrine like that of Descartes, or of Leibnitz himself, we always imply that the will follows, more or less, from the understanding or at least accompanies it, so that when God creates he knows precisely what he is creating. Thus, the conception of man in the mind of God is comparable to that of the paper-knife in the mind of the artisan: God makes man according to a procedure and a conception, exactly as the artisan manufactures a paper-knife, following a definition and a formula. Thus each individual man is the realisation of a certain conception which dwells in the divine understanding. In the philosophic atheism of the eighteenth century, the notion of God is suppressed, but not, for all that, the idea that essence is prior to existence; something of that idea we still find everywhere in Diderot, in Voltaire and even in Kant. Man possesses a human nature; that 'human nature', which is the conception of human being, is found in every man; which means that each man is a particular example of an universal conception, the conception of Man. In Kant, this universality goes so far that the wild man of the woods, man in the state of nature and the bourgeois are all contained in the same definition and have the same fundamental qualities. Here again, the essence of man precedes that historic existence which we confront in experience.

Atheistic existentialism, of which I am a representative, declares with greater consistency that if God does not exist there is at least one being whose existence comes before its essence, a being which exists before it can be defined by any conception of it. That being is man or, as Heidegger has it, the human reality. What do we mean by saying that existence precedes essence? We mean that man first of all exists, encounters himself, surges up in the world—and defines himself afterwards. If man as the existentialist sees him is not definable, it is because to begin with he is nothing. He will not be anything until later, and then he will be what he makes of himself. Thus, there is no human nature, because there is no God to have a conception of it. Man simply is. Not that he is simply what he conceives himself to be, but he is what he wills, and as he conceives himself after already existing—as he wills to be after that leap towards existence.

Existentialism and Humanism (1946)

In Possession of Self

That is the first principle of existentialism. And this is what people call its 'subjectivity' using the word as a reproach against us. But what do we mean to say by this, but that man is of a greater dignity than a stone or a table? For we mean to say that man primarily exists—that man is, before all else, something which propels itself towards a future and is aware that it is doing so. Man is, indeed, a project which possesses a subject life, instead of being a kind of moss, or a fungus or a cauliflower. Before that projection of the self nothing exists; not even in the heaven of intelligence: man will only attain existence when he is what he purposes to be. Not, however, what he may wish to be. For what we usually understand by wishing or willing is a conscious decision taken—much more often than not—after we have made ourselves what we are. I may wish to join a party, to write a book or to marry—but in such a case what is usually called my will is probably a manifestation of a prior and more spontaneous decision. If, however, it is true that existence is prior to essence, man is responsible for what he is. Thus, the first effect of existentialism is that it puts every man in possession of himself as he is, and places the entire responsibility for his existence squarely upon his own shoulders. And, when we say that man is responsible for himself, we do not mean that he is responsible only for his own individuality, but that he is responsible for all men.

Ibid.

A. J. AYER
1910–1989

The Foundation of Morality

The hostility of the rationalists to religious dogmatism was not evinced only in their fidelity to the natural sciences. It extended also to questions of human conduct. This did not mean that their moral principles were necessarily different from those which were held by their religious antagonists. The difference lay in their denying that morality either had a religious basis or needed a religious sanction.

In maintaining that one cannot look to religion to supply a logical foundation for any code of morality, they were demonstrably right. The decisive argument in their favour is that no moral system can rest solely on authority. It can never be a sufficient justification for performing any action that someone wishes or commands it. Not only has it first to be established that the person in question has a legitimate claim on one's allegiance, but even when this has been established, it still does not necessarily follow that what he commands is right. Neither does it make any difference to the argument whether the authority is taken to be human or divine. No doubt the premiss that what God wills is right is one that religious believers take for granted. The fact remains that even if they were justified in making this assumption, it implies that they have a standard of morality which is independent of their belief in God. The proof of this is that when they say that God is good or that he wills what is right, they surely do not mean merely to express the tautology that he is what he is or that he wills what he wills. If they did mean no more than this, they would be landed with the absurd consequence that even if the actions of the deity were such as, in any other person, we should characterize as those of a malignant demon, they would still, by definition, be right. But the fact is that believers in God think of the goodness which they attribute to him as something for which we ought to be grateful. Now this would make no sense at all if the deity's volition set the standard of value: for in that case, no matter what he was understood to will, we should still be obliged to think him good.

It is no answer to this argument to say that the possibility of God's being anything other than good is excluded by his nature. There is, indeed, no logical objection to building goodness into the definition of God so long as it is compatible with the other attributes which go to make up the concept. The drawback is only that it adds to the difficulty of supposing that the concept is satisfied. But so far from this proving that God's nature can serve to define goodness, it proves just the opposite. If one did not know what one understood by goodness, independently of ascribing it to God, its inclusion in the definition would not be intelligible.

Not only is it a fallacy to think that moral principles can logically depend upon the will of God: it is also a fallacy to look to human morality for a proof of God's existence. The underlying assumption is that only purely selfish behaviour is natural to man; so that if it ever happens, as it not infrequently does, that people behave unselfishly, they must be inspired by a higher power. But . . . this assumption is false and the conclusion which is drawn from it is invalid. The assumption is false because the only criterion for deciding what is natural to man is what men actually do. Antecedently to experience, there can be no reason for expecting people to behave in one way rather than another. If experience shows that they act unselfishly as well as selfishly, we can only conclude that both types of behaviour are natural. No doubt the self-regarding impulses are the stronger, and in many persons remain so, but this does not alter the fact that many actions are motivated by concern for others. If the capacity for evil is part of human nature, so is the capacity for good.

The Humanist Outlook (1968)

PETER MEDAWAR
1915–1987

Views of a Rationalist Scientist

To abdicate from the rule of reason and substitute for it an authentication of belief by the intentness and degree of conviction with which we hold it can be perilous and destructive. Religious belief gives a spurious spiritual dimension to tribal enmities, as we see them in the Low Countries, Ceylon, Northern Ireland and parts of Africa; nor has any religious belief been held with greater passion or degree of conviction than the metaphysics of blood and soil which did so much to animate Hitler's Germany. Was that not also a consequence of just such a deep, passionate conviction as that which has been thought to authenticate religious belief?

The problem of pain has not been solved, though it has been almost hidden from view by a cloud of theological humbug and the still greater exertions of doublethink that conceal from view or pretend the nonexistence of the most unwelcome truth of all. It goes with the passionate intensity and deep conviction of the truth of a religious belief, and of course of the importance of the superstitious observances that go with it, that we should want others to share it—and the only certain way to cause a religious belief to be held by everyone is to liquidate nonbelievers. The price in blood and tears that mankind generally has had to pay for the comfort and spiritual refreshment that religion has brought to a few has been too great to justify our entrusting moral accountancy to religious belief. By 'moral accountancy' I mean the judgement that such and such an action is right or wrong, or such a man good and such another evil.

I am a rationalist—something of a period piece nowadays, I admit—but I am usually reluctant to declare myself to be so because of the widespread misunderstanding or neglect of the distinction that must always be drawn in philosophic discussion between the *sufficient* and the *necessary*. I do not believe— indeed, I deem it a comic blunder to believe—that the exercise of reason is *sufficient* to explain our condition and where necessary to remedy it, but I do believe that the world can be made a better place to live in—believe, indeed, that it has already been made so by an endeavour in which, in spite of shortcomings which I do not conceal, natural science has played an important part, of which my fellow scientists and I are immensely proud. I fear that we may never be able to answer those questions about first and last things that have been the subject of this short essay—questions to do with the origin, purpose and destiny of man; we know, however, that whether as individuals or as political people, we do have some say in what comes next, so what could our destiny be except what we make it?

To people of sanguine temperament, the thought that this is so is a source of strength and the energizing force of a just and honourable ambition.

The dismay that may be aroused by our inability to answer questions about first and last things is something for which ordinary people have long since worked out for themselves Voltaire's remedy: 'We must cultivate our garden.'

The Limits of Science (1986)

ALEXANDER COMFORT
1920–

Can Science Make us Good?

Man has a great fear of loneliness, and he has, we know, a very strong tendency to personalize his surroundings—to put a mind like his own into them. One of our difficulties in studying animals is to get over this idea that they are human persons; many cultures don't even try to do so and they ascribe to birds, bears, trees, the weather, human minds and emotions. In our own advertisements furniture, locomotives and even things like meat pies appear with faces. If we draw a face on an inanimate object we find it in some sense easier to make contact with it. It would not be surprising if men tended to draw faces on the Universe as a whole. Less sophisticated men have seen the whole of nature as peopled with numbers of deities and spirits—more sophisticated cultures have reduced the number: the only consistent feature of such faces is the striking likeness they have borne to the people who drew them.

The humanist view of these faces is that they are reflections of the human face. The view of most of the major religions is that they are real, and that there is, or are, one or more personal intelligences, gods, which offer some form of co-operation to man, and make ritual and moral demands on him.

Neither of those views seems to me directly demonstrable. I am not sure that for my purposes they need be, so far as all-or-none demonstration is concerned. It used to be thought that smallpox was caused by an offended demon. But it hasn't in fact ever been necessary to devise an experiment to prove that it is not, and I don't think one could devise such an experiment. What has been done is to show, over a long period of time, that another set of assumptions makes it possible to control smallpox reliably. As a result it no longer seems necessary or important to consider a demonic origin for it. There has been a steady reduction throughout human history in the number of practical matters in which the intervention of a God is really expected to occur, even by religious people, and the success of human control over nature has run parallel with the extent to which we have recognized that it won't. Each practical success in dealing with the problems of things has usually meant one further reduction in the field where animistic and intuitive ideas still held good—and they have gone, as a rule, not by a process of formal disproof but simply through losing their intellectual meaning when they lost their possible use. They have not in most cases been disproved so much as outgrown, but when they are supported that process is slow. I have sometimes imagined the kind of literature which might exist in our culture if one of the most deepseated and comforting tenets embodied in our traditional religion had been the real existence of mermaids. It would be no good, I think, pointing out that they were improbable organisms, counter to almost everything we know about vertebrates, or that legends of this kind are general among savages, or that supposed mermaids were probably dugongs. We would still be told in sermons that humanity by its nature cries out for the reality of mermaids, that we need only believe and we should see them with our own eyes— which is quite true—that the seas were full of surprises and coelacanths, and that no biologist could prove that it did not also contain mermaids. At the last ditch we should be told that they exist in a symbolic manner. If moreover any authority, however antimermaid he might be, were to express the view that there might be marine organisms unknown to science, a paean would go up that science was returning to the faith of its fathers.

The issue of supernaturalism versus humanism is more complex than that of the existence of mermaids and more important, but the case for humanism and the case against mermaids do have a very great deal in common. I didn't want to argue it on quite the lines upon which it has so often been argued. I think future belief in this matter will be determined as our belief over smallpox or over mermaids has been determined in the past— less by formal proofs than by the consequences of coping with practical problems. I have in mind the particular problem of the control of human conduct. I put in the second half of my title— 'Can science make us good?'—to focus our discussion, if I may, on this point.

The reason it was important to stop attributing smallpox to devils was that this belief interfered with our chances of control-ling it. It made us waste our time. Now disease and physical threats from his environment are among the problems which man has been confronting throughout his development. Perhaps the most important human achievement so far has been the devel-opment of a technique for dealing with them, the scientific method. In controlling the physical world it has worked. The ques-tion now arises of its application to the other major group of human problems, those which come from human conduct. Over this, we are now where medicine was when the demonic origin of smallpox was under debate. It has long been said that human conduct problems are not of the same kind as problems in the physical world, that they have a supernatural quality which makes them insoluble in humanistic terms. Hippocrates wrote about epilepsy, 'This is termed the holy sickness, but I see no reason to regard it as more holy than any other illness.' I am going to sug-gest to you that human moral conduct is not a holy subject, but an investigable and rational one.

There are as I see it two main issues between humanist and supernaturalist over this. The first is whether humanism is capa-ble of providing values by which conduct can be judged—and the second is whether human beings, granted the acceptance of eth-ical values, are capable of realizing them without supernatural intervention. This second question is, in fact, or ought to be, something which can be settled experimentally.

We have rather evidently reached the point at which human achievement is being limited not by lack of control over nature but by social and psychological factors in human societies. It is said, sometimes, I'm afraid, with something approaching satisfaction, that the outcome of science is itself threatening man with destruc-tion, and that this is a divine judgement on arrogance—man can control nuclear energy but he cannot control himself. Now humanity might in fact be destroyed or seriously damaged by the products of technology—either by accident, or through its present habit of allowing its societies to be governed by mentally diseased people. But if it is, the reason will be its failure to apply sufficiently quickly to the form of its own societies the methods it has already applied to the control of nature.

When we hear it said that science has already failed to make us good, I always want to draw attention to the time-scale of things. There have been recognizable men for about a million years. There have been fairly highly developed human societies (I stand to be corrected on this) for about twelve thousand years. If we date the description of the scientific method from Bacon, then it has been in existence for three hundred years. It has been seriously applied to medicine and natural sciences for about two hundred years with the results we know. It has been applied to human social behaviour for eighty to a hundred years. In that time it has already produced a greater revolution both in human awareness and, I think it is true to say, in human ethics, than religion has produced in several centuries—and its rate of progress in all these fields tends to be exponential; it is likely to go faster the farther it moves. . . .

We have not made man good by science, but in the last ten or twenty years we have learned, first that he can be made good, by relatively simple adjustments in ways of living, and secondly, enough about the nature of his behaviour to leave no doubt, in my mind at least, that we are in possession of the only key which is likely to solve the problem. If we don't by this means succeed in avoiding the dangers of the time, there is nothing in history to suggest that any other prescription would have been better able to do so. For we have already, to my mind, in our limited application of psychology and social science to problems of conduct, got better results in a very short time than the supernatural moralities have produced in a very much longer run. . . .

I will try to deal later on with the validity and competence of values devised solely from human sources. The humanistic values are, I believe, largely related to techniques. 'Morals' dictated by values of this sort are effectively techniques of living, not moral laws. Bertrand Russell called them 'conditions of happiness'.

They obviously won't always be easy to define or adhere to. In the past, gods and supernatural beliefs have been of importance to morals not so much by giving us revelation as by giving us motivation. If, as I think, we must obtain our revelation by research, we do need to replace that motivation with one as strong. And I wonder whether we won't find it largely in the very awareness that we are alone—that, as Sherrington said at the end of *Man on his Nature,* 'we have because human, an inalienable prerogative of responsibility which we cannot devolve . . . we can share it only with each other.'

'The Case for Humanism—or Can Science Make Us Good?'
(Opening contribution to a discussion before the
Fifty-One Society, broadcast in 1957)

ANTONY FLEW
1923–

The Presumption of Atheism

What does show the presumption of atheism to be the right one is what we have now to investigate.

An obvious first move is to appeal to the old legal axiom: '*Ei incumbit probatio qui dicit, non qui negat.*' Literally and unsympathetically translated this becomes: 'The onus of proof lies on the man who affirms, not on the man who denies.' To this the objection is almost equally obvious. Given just a very little verbal ingenuity, the content of any motion can be rendered alternatively in either a negative or a positive form: either, 'That this house affirms the existence of God'; or, 'That this house takes its stand for positive atheism'. So interpreted, therefore, our axiom provides no determinate guidance.

Suppose, however, that we take the hint already offered in the previous paragraph. A less literal but more sympathetic translation would be: 'The onus of proof lies on the proposition, not on the opposition.' The point of the change is to bring out that this maxim was offered in a legal context, and that our courts are institutions of debate. An axiom providing no determinate guidance outside that framework may nevertheless be fundamental for the

effective conduct of orderly and decisive debate. Here the outcome is supposed to be decided on the merits of what is said
within the debate itself, and of that alone. So no opposition can
set about demolishing the proposition case until and unless that
proposition has first provided them with a case for demolition:
'You've got to get something on your plate before you can start
messing it around.'

Of course our maxim even when thus sympathetically interpreted still offers no direction on which contending parties ought
to be made to undertake which roles. Granting that courts are to
operate as debating institutions, and granting that this maxim is
fundamental to debate, we have to appeal to some further
premise principle before we become licensed to infer that the
prosecution must propose and the defence oppose. This further
principle is, once again, the familiar presumption of innocence.
Were we, while retaining the conception of a court as an institution for reaching decisions by way of formalised debate, to
embrace the opposition presumption, the presumption of guilt, we
should need to adopt the opposite arrangements. In these the
defence would first propose that the accused is after all innocent,
and the prosecution would then respond by struggling to disinte-
grate the case proposed.

The first move examined cannot, therefore, be by itself sufficient. To have considered it does nevertheless help to show that
to accept such a presumption is to adopt a policy. And policies
have to be assessed by reference to the aims of those for whom
they are suggested. If for you it is more important that no guilty
person should ever be acquitted than that no innocent person
should ever be convicted, then for you a presumption of guilt
must be the rational policy. For you, with your preference structure, a presumption of innocence becomes simply irrational. To
adopt this policy would be to adopt means calculated to frustrate
your own chosen ends; which is, surely, paradigmatically irrational. Take, as an actual illustration, the controlling elite of a rul-
ing Leninist party, which must as such refuse to recognise any
individual rights if these conflict with the claims of the party, and
which in fact treats all those suspected of actual or potential
opposition much as if they were already known 'counter-revolu-
tionaries', 'enemies of socialism', 'friends of the United States',

'advocates of free elections', and all other like things bad. I can, and do, fault this policy and its agents on many counts. Yet I cannot say that for them, once granted their scale of values, it is irrational.

What then are the aims by reference to which an atheist presumption might be justified? One key word in the answer, if not the key word, must be 'knowledge'. The context for which such a policy is proposed is that of inquiry about the existence of God; and the object of the exercise is, presumably, to discover whether it is possible to establish that the word 'God' does in fact have application. Now to establish must here be either to show that you know or to come to know. But knowledge is crucially different from mere true belief. All knowledge involves true belief; not all true belief constitutes knowledge. To have a true belief is simply and solely to believe that something is so, and to be in fact right. But someone may believe that this or that is so, and his belief may in fact be true, without its thereby and necessarily constituting knowledge. If a true belief is to achieve this more elevated status, then the believer has to be properly warranted so to believe. He must, that is, be in a position to know.

Obviously there is enormous scope for disagreement in particular cases: both about what is required in order to be in a position to know; and about whether these requirements have actually been satisfied. But the crucial distinction between believing truly and knowing is recognised as universally as the prior and equally vital distinction between believing and believing what is in fact true. If, for instance, there is a question whether a colleague performed some discreditable action, then all of us, though we have perhaps to admit that we cannot help believing that he did, are rightly scrupulous not to assert that this is known unless we have grounds sufficient to warrant the bolder claim. It is, therefore, not only incongruous but also scandalous in matters of life and death, and even of eternal life and death, to maintain that you know either on no grounds at all, or on grounds of a kind which on other and comparatively minor issues you yourself would insist to be inadequate.

It is by reference to this inescapable demand for grounds that the presumption of atheism is justified. If it is to be established that there is a God, then we have to have good grounds for believing that this is indeed so. Until and unless some such grounds are produced we have literally no reason at all for believing; and in that situation the only reasonable posture must be that of either the negative atheist or the agnostic. So the onus of proof has to rest on the proposition. It must be up to them: first, to give whatever sense they choose to the word 'God', meeting any objection that so defined it would relate only to an incoherent-pseudo-concept; and, second, to bring forward sufficient reasons to warrant their claim that, in their present sense of the word 'God', there is a God. The same applies, with appropriate alterations, if what is to be made out is, not that theism is known to be true, but only—more modestly—that it can be seen to be at least more or less probable.

The Presumption of Atheism (1975)

PAUL KURTZ
1925–

A Moral Revolution

Humanists have been debating for years the proper definition of humanism. It is clear that humanism is not a dogma or creed and that there are many varieties of, and meanings given to, humanism. Nevertheless, one may suggest at least four characteristics that contemporary humanists emphasize.

First, humanists have some confidence in man and they believe that the only bases for morality are human experience and human needs. Second, many or most humanists are opposed to all forms of supernaturalistic and authoritarian religion. Third, many humanists believe that scientific intelligence and critical reason can assist in reconstructing our moral values. And fourth, humanism is humanitarian in that it is concerned with the good life and social justice as moral ideals.

Humanism as a movement is wide enough to include many people who will agree with some of the above points, but not all. What characterizes an increasing number of people is a commitment to a moral point of view in which mankind is viewed as a whole. Such a characteristic does not make one a humanist by itself. Yet, it is an ideal that most humanists share. Humanists may honestly disagree about their political beliefs and about many social questions. There is no humanist party line. What humanists today share in common, however, are a concern for humanity, a belief that moral values must be removed from the mantle of theological dogma, and a conviction that our moral ideals must be constantly re-examined and revised in the light of present needs and social demands.

The present epoch is a revolutionary one, involving a radical questioning of basic foundations, structures, beliefs and values. In the present context humanism has become especially identified with the moral revolution. It is this aspect that I wish to focus upon.

There have been many kinds of revolution in human history: political, economic, social, scientific. The revolution that we are experiencing today is a moral revolution. Although it has many dimensions, at its roots the revolution is humanistic. It involves a critique of religious, ideological and moralistic philosophies that tend to deny or denigrate the most genuine qualities of human existence. And it is an attempt to recover those human aspects of life that have been lost in post-industrial society.

The overthrow of customary morality has occurred in large part because of an explosive technology that has rapidly transformed our culture. A sharp disparity has emerged between the new technology and our inherited moral codes. The latter were encased in custom, enshrined in sacred tradition and supported by the sanction of law. The moral tradition was taken as absolute—unquestionable and beyond the range of critical inquiry. The strains between the received morality and the demands of modern life were too great; the moral 'virtues' were out of touch with the world and practice deviated widely from professed ideals.

Suddenly, the dam has burst and the old moral mythology is now being lampooned. There is a long-overdue demand for reappraisal and modification. A moral reconstruction is proceeding at an accelerated pace.

There are both negative and positive aspects to the current moral reformation. It involves a devastating critique of the hypocrisy and injustice of the Establishment, but it also involves a creative effort to develop new moral ideals more appropriate to the world in which we live. Several ideals are being proclaimed at the same time. These are often unclear and confused.

The basic assumption of the new morality is the conviction that the good life is achieved when we realize the human potential. This means that we ought to reject all those creeds and dogmas that impede human fulfilment or impose external authoritarian rules upon human beings. The traditional supernaturalistic moral commandments are especially repressive of our human needs. They are immoral insofar as they foster illusions about human destiny and suppress vital inclinations.

The moral revolution rejects those impersonal bureaucratic organizations that smother individuality and restrict human autonomy. The new morality is appreciative of the fact that modern technology has provided great benefits for the good life—that it has helped to eliminate the scourges of disease, hunger, drudgery and misery. But the new morality is especially critical of the dehumanizing and depersonalizing aspects of technology. It attacks the fact that man increasingly tends to lose his sense of responsibility and his appetite for creativity in the highly complex society in which we now live. Human alienation is accentuated by the banality of a consumer-oriented, manipulative economic system that conditions false desires and needs.

Thus the humanistic revolution seeks to rescue the positive qualities of life experience; it seeks to rediscover joy and love, creativity and growth, shared experiences and fraternity, uniqueness and diversity, achievement and excellence. These are human goods that must be cultivated anew if we are to overcome the blind forces that threaten the quality of life. A significant life, which fuses pleasure and creative self-realization, is possible, says the humanist, and men can again discover ways of enriching experience, actualizing potentialities and achieving happiness. But if human experience is to flower it is essential that normative principles prevail in our social life.

The Humanist Alternative (1973)

RICHARD DAWKINS
1941–

Viruses of the Mind

Like computer viruses, successful mind viruses will tend to be hard for their victims to detect. If you are the victim of one, the chances are that you won't know it, and may even vigorously deny it. Accepting that a virus might be difficult to detect in your own mind, what tell-tale signs might you look out for? I shall answer by imagining how a medical textbook might describe the typical symptoms of a sufferer (arbitrarily assumed to be male).

1. The patient typically finds himself impelled by some deep, inner conviction that something is true, or right, or virtuous: a conviction that doesn't seem to owe anything to evidence or reason, but which, nevertheless, he feels as totally compelling and convincing. We doctors refer to such a belief as 'faith'.

2. Patients typically make a positive virtue of faith's being strong and unshakeable, in spite of not being based upon evidence. Indeed, they may feel that the less the evidence there is, the more virtuous the belief.

This paradoxical idea that lack of evidence is a positive virtue where faith is concerned has something of the quality of a program that is self-sustaining, because it is self-referential. Once the proposition is believed, it automatically undermines opposition to itself. The 'lack of evidence is a virtue' idea would be an admirable sidekick, ganging up with faith itself in a clique of mutually supportive viral programs.

3. A related symptom, which a faith-sufferer may also present, is the conviction that 'mystery,' *per se,* is a good thing. It is not a virtue to solve mysteries. Rather we should enjoy them, even revel in their insolubility.

Any impulse to solve mysteries could be seriously inimical to the spread of a mind virus. It would not, therefore, be surprising if the idea that 'mysteries are better not solved' was a favoured member of a mutually supporting gang of viruses. Take the 'Mystery of the Transubstantiation'. It is easy and nonmysterious to believe that in some symbolic or metaphorical sense the eucharistic wine turns into the blood of Christ. The Roman

Catholic doctrine of transubstantiation, however, claims far more. The 'whole substance' of the wine is converted into 'the blood of Christ'; the appearance of wine that remains is 'merely accidental', 'inhering in no substance'. Transubstantiation is colloquially taught as meaning that the wine 'literally' turns into the blood of Christ. Whether in its obfuscatory Aristotelian or its franker colloquial form, the claim of transubstantiation can be made only if we do serious violence to the normal meanings of words like 'substance' and 'literally'. Redefining words is not a sin but, if we use words like 'whole substance' and 'literally' for this case, what word are we going to use when we really and truly want to say that something did actually happen? As Anthony Kenny observed of his own puzzlement as a young seminarian, 'For all I could tell, my typewriter might be Benjamin Disraeli transubstantiated. . . .'

Viruses of the Mind (1992)

JACOB BRONOWSKI
1908–1974

The Itch for the Absolute

There are two parts to the human dilemma. One is the belief that the end justifies the means. That push-button philosophy, that deliberate deafness to suffering, has become the monster in the war machine. The other is the betrayal of the human spirit: the assertion of dogma that closes the mind, and turns a nation, a civilisation, into a regiment of ghosts, obedient ghosts, or tortured ghosts.

It is said that science will dehumanise people and turn them into numbers. That is false, tragically false. Look for yourself. This is the concentration camp and crematorium at Auschwitz. This is where people were turned into numbers. Into this pond were flushed the ashes of some four million people. And that was not done by gas. It was done by arrogance. It was done by dogma. It was done by ignorance. When people believe that they have absolute knowledge, with no test in reality, this is how they behave. This is what men do when they aspire to the knowledge of gods.

Science is a very human form of knowledge. We are always at the brink of the known, we always feel forward for what is to be hoped. Every judgment in science stands on the edge of error, and is personal. Science is a tribute to what we can know although we are fallible. In the end the words were said by Oliver Cromwell: 'I beseech you, in the bowels of Christ, think it possible you may be mistaken.'

I owe it as a scientist to my friend Leo Szilard, I owe it as a human being to the many members of my family who died at Auschwitz, to stand here by the pond as a survivor and a witness. We have to cure ourselves of the itch for absolute knowledge and power. We have to close the distance between the push-button order and the human act. We have to touch people.

The Ascent of Man **(1973)**

DAVID ATTENBOROUGH
1926–

Human Responsibilities

Man's passion to communicate and to receive communications seems as central to his success as a species as the fin was to the fish or the feather to the birds. We do not limit ourselves to our own acquaintances or even our own generation. Archaeologists labour to decipher clay tablets rescued with painstaking care from Uruk and other ancient cities in the hope that the same citizen long ago may have recorded a message of more significance than a boastful genealogy of a chief or a laundry list. In our own cities, dignitaries arrange for messages to be sent to future generations by burying writings in steel cylinders strong enough to survive even a nuclear catastrophe. And scientists, convinced that man's most refined language of all is that of mathematics, select a universal truth that they believe will be recognised through all eternity—a formula for the wavelength of light—and beam it towards other galaxies in the Milky Way to proclaim that here on earth, after three thousand million years of evolution, a creature has emerged that has for the first time devised its own way of accumulating and transferring experience across generations.

This last chapter has been devoted to only one species, ourselves. This may have given the impression that somehow man is the ultimate triumph of evolution, that all these millions of years of development have had no purpose other than to put him on earth. There is no scientific evidence whatever to support such a view and no reason to suppose that our stay here will be any more permanent than that of the dinosaur. The processes of evolution are still going on among plants and birds, insects and mammals. So it is more than likely that if men were to disappear from the face of the earth, for whatever reason, there is a modest, unobtrusive creature somewhere that would develop into a new form and take our place.

But although denying that we have a special position in the natural world might seem becomingly modest in the eye of eternity, it might also be used as an excuse for evading our responsibilities. The fact is that no species has ever had such wholesale control over everything on earth, living or dead, as we now have. That lays upon us, whether we like it or not, an awesome responsibility. In our hands now lies not only our own future, but that of all other living creatures with whom we share the earth.

Life on Earth (1979)

APPENDIX

CONFUCIUS (551–479 B.C.) Latin for K'ung Fu-tzu, the master of K'ung. After becoming a government official with a retinue of followers, he had a successful ministerial career. After a breach with the ruler, he spent 12 years as an itinerant sage, then settled in his later years spending his time teaching and writing. The *Analects* are the most comprehensive account of his sayings. He replaced religious teachings with moral values.

THUCYDIDES (c. 460–401 B.C.) A Greek historian, who commanded a squadron of Athenian ships, but failed in his task and took refuge after a death sentence. In exile he wrote his *History of the Peloponnesian War.* He aimed at a rational and impartial account of history.

EPICURUS (342–270 B.C.) A Greek philosopher, who taught many followers in his school in the community of the Garden. Only a few fragments of his works remain, but his ideas were relayed by Cicero, Plutarch and especially Lucretius. He aimed to promote detachment and serenity, creating the absence of pain by a simple and temperate life. He adopted a materialistic view of the universe.

MENCIUS (fl. late 4th century B.C.) Latin for Meng-Tze, who was the most important successor of Confucius in the Chinese tradition of pragmatic moral philosophy. He gathered a group of disciples and travelled around the empire trying in vain to find a ruler who would put his principles of moderate conservatism into practice. The writings attributed to him were collected in a book bearing his name, which is one of the classics of Chinese thought.

CICERO (106–43 B.C.) He was a Roman man of action, orator and essayist. He took a full part in military and political life during a turbulent period of Roman history. One of his most famous speeches was the *Phillipic* against Marcus Antonius, which lost him his life. Among his works were *On Duties* and *On the Nature of the Gods.*

LUCRETIUS (c. 99–55 B.C.) A Roman poet and philosopher. His major work was *On the Nature of Things,* a long poem, which presented the views of Democritus and Epicurus. It denounced religion as a source of human misery. He proposed a calm mind and a materialistic philosophy.

SENECA (c. 4 B.C.–A.D. 65) A Roman philosopher and statesman, also a dramatist. His career was damaged by being banished by Claudius, for alleged adultery with his niece. On his return he became tutor to Nero, but failed to teach him philosophy or morality. During Nero's rule he was ordered to commit suicide, which he did—following his philosophy—stoically.

PLINY THE ELDER (A.D. 23–79) A Roman soldier and writer. He wrote a history of the German wars, but was much interested in scientific and natural phenomena. He was friendly with the Emperor Vespasian, but did not allow court life to stop him writing. He wrote 160 volumes of an encyclopaedia, *Natural History*—which remains a rich source of information about Roman times.

PLUTARCH (c. A.D. 46–120) A Greek historian and biographer, who spent most of his life in his native Athens. Two of his most notable biographical works were *Parallel Lives* and *Biographies,* which provide an accurate record of the figures of his time or the period immediately preceding him. *Morals* comprised a variety of writings on ethical issues.

EPICTETUS (1st century A.D.) A Greek slave in Rome, who gained his freedom and taught philosophy. He was, like many philosophers, banished in 90 and went to Epirus. His sayings were collected. He was a Stoic philosopher who taught submission to fate, self-abnegation, and love of one's enemies.

MARCUS AURELIUS ANTONINUS (A.D.121–180) A successful and admired Roman Emperor, whose *Meditations* are among the very few writings to be preserved from a Roman Emperor. Although a man of peace, his emperorship was beset with frontier wars. He was a Stoic, with a gentle and detached state of mind, who believed: 'A happy lot and portion is good inclinations of the soul, good desires, good actions.'

CELSUS (2nd century A.D.) A Roman philosopher whose writings are anti-Jewish and anti-Christian. Much of his work was destroyed when the Roman Empire became Christian.

IBN RUSHD (AVERROËS) (1126–1198) Born in Cordova, he became the most famous of medieval Islamic philosophers. He was a judge who wrote on jurisprudence. He was advisor to the Caliph, but later banished from court by his son. He lived in retirement in Marrakesh. His major work is the *Commentaries on Aristotle.* He was an important source of Greek and Arabic thought to Christian philosophers.

MICHEL EYQUEM DE MONTAIGNE (1533–1592) A noted humanist writer and essayist. He studied the classics and then law. He took part in public life in Bordeaux as city counsellor. He then retired to his tower, where he wrote his *Essays.* He was a sceptic and critical of warring religions. On the wall of his study were the words: *'Homo sum, humani a me nihil alienum puto'* (I am a man, I consider nothing human to be alien to me—Terence).

GIORDANO BRUNO (1548–1600) An Italian philosopher and scientist. He was an unorthodox Dominican Friar, who travelled widely teaching and lecturing. He developed a pantheistic philosophy and supported Copernicus in his cosmological theories. He was brought before the Inquisition for his adherence to Copernican theories and after a seven-year trial was burned at the stake.

BENEDICT SPINOZA (1632–1677) He came from a Portuguese Jewish family, which took refuge in Amsterdam. He was interested in optics and mathematics and eventually earned his living as a lens grinder. His writings on religion advocated a strict historical approach to the Bible and freedom of speech in religious matters. He was expelled from his synagogue and denounced as an atheist, although believing in a pantheistic divinity. His last work *Ethics* derived moral behaviour from rational sources.

JEAN MESLIER (1664–1729) A *curé* who spent his life in the Ardennes where he was born. He combined his role as a priest with the writing of a vehement criticism of Christianity and proof of the absence of God. In his *Testament* he argued that religion is a human invention and that the natural order did not require a sovereign deity. It was not published in full until the nineteenth century.

VOLTAIRE (François Marie Arouet) (1694–1778) The polymath of the Enlightenment, he wrote plays, poetry, history, science, *contes* and polemical satires—for which he is perhaps best remembered. In a visit to England he became influenced by the theories of Locke and the observation of religious toleration; he later wrote the *Traité sur la Tolérance*. Among his most influential works were the *Dictionnaire Philosophique,* with its satirical undercurrent, and *Candide,* which is accepted as a masterpiece.

DAVID HUME (1711–1776) A Scottish philosopher, he was renowned as a writer and popular as a man of great good humour. His first philosophic work *A Treatise on Human Nature* fell flat, but he later rewrote it in more digestible form as an *Inquiry Concerning Human Understanding.* His suspected atheism denied him university posts, and he made a living writing—especially with his *History of England.* His *Dialogues concerning Natural Religion* were published posthumously, since they contain clear evidence of his sceptical stance towards religion.

DENIS DIDEROT (1713–1784) A key figure in the French Enlightenment. His early works brought him trouble: his *Pensées Philosophiques* was burned by the Paris parlement in 1746 and in 1749 he was imprisoned for his *Lettre sur les Aveugles.* His life work was the editorship of the *Encyclopédie,* which brought him constantly to the edge of prosecution. The *Encyclopédie* aimed to cover all arts and sciences, but a counter theme was an agenda of scepticism and satire on religion.

PAUL HENRI THIRY D'HOLBACH (1723–1789) Born in Germany, he became a French *philosophe.* He was a leading contributor (mainly on scientific subjects) to the *Encyclopédie.* He was among the first avowed atheist writers. Many of his works were issued pseudonymously. *Christianity Unveiled* was a fiercely critical 'Examination of the principles and effects of the Christian religion'. *System of Nature* (1770) was a materialistic account of the universe.

ADAM SMITH (1723–1790) A member of the Scottish Enlightenment, who knew Hume well. He is most famous for his works on political economy, his masterpiece being *Inquiry into the Nature and Causes of the Wealth of Nations.*

EDWARD GIBBON (1737–1794) He came from the family of a country gentleman. His education in classics and history was a good preparation for his major work *The Decline and Fall of the Roman Empire.* The two chapters on the rise of the Christians and the Roman conduct towards the Christians became notorious—to indignant clerics and to enthusiastic freethinkers.

THOMAS PAINE (1737–1809) He was a major figure in the radical movements of the eighteenth century, taking part in the American Revolution and the French Revolution. His major works are *Rights of Man* and, although he was a deist, a blistering attack on revealed religion, *The Age of Reason.*

CONDORCET (1743–1794) A mathematician and *philosophe,* he contributed articles to Diderot's *Encyclopédie.* He took part in the French Revolution and became president of the Legislative Assembly for a period. He was later imprisoned, and at this time wrote *Sketch for a Historical Picture of the Progress of the Human Mind.*

JEREMY BENTHAM (1748–1832) He was a philosopher and social reformer, who founded London University. He developed the utilitarian idea of the aim of behaviour and legislation being to benefit the 'greatest happiness of the greatest number'.

WILLIAM GODWIN (1756–1836) He was a novelist and philosopher who started as a Calvinist minister, but became a 'complete unbeliever'. *Enquiry Concerning Political Justice* (1793) created a strong impression, especially on the young Shelley, who married his daughter by Mary Wollstonecraft. His best novel was *Caleb Williams.*

ARTHUR SCHOPENHAUER (1788–1860) German philosopher of pessimistic temperament, who opposed the idealist views of Hegel. He was inspired by Plato, Goethe and Indian philosophy. His major work is *The World as Will and Idea* (1819).

PERCY BYSSHE SHELLEY (1792–1822) He was a poet and political activist. He was expelled from Oxford University for coauthoring with Thomas Jefferson Hogg *The Necessity of Atheism.* An early poem, *Queen Mab,* was ferociously critical of religion and influenced nineteenth-century radicals. He spent the later part of his life in Italy, where he wrote his great odes and *Prometheus Unbound.*

HEINRICH HEINE (1797–1856) A Jewish German who was educated in banking and the law, but who preferred to write poetry and essays of travel and politics. After quarrelling with German radicals, he lived for many years in France, eventually being confined to his bed, while continuing to write great poems.

AUGUSTE MARIE FRANÇOIS XAVIER COMTE (1798–1857) He studied at the École Polytechnique in Paris and was influenced by the socialist Saint-Simon. He developed his own attitude to religion in 'Positivism', a religion without God. His ideas are set out at length in *The Course of Political Positivism* and *System of Political Positivism.* He influenced J. S. Mill and George Eliot.

LUDWIG ANDREAS FEUERBACH (1804–1872) He was a German philosopher, who reacted against Hegel's 'idealism'. His major work was *The Essence of Christianity,* which was translated into English by George Eliot. Christianity was criticised and religion seen as a human dream. His materialism influenced Marx.

JOHN STUART MILL (1806–1873) His father, James Mill, subjected him to very early precocious education. He was in the utilitarian tradition, but he modified that view considerably. His reputation was established by *A System of Logic* (1843). Two of his major works are *On Liberty* (1859) and *The Subjection of Women* (1869).

CHARLES DARWIN (1809–1882) The man who first put forward the theory of evolution by natural selection, after a tour on HMS Beagle to the Galapagos Islands. His *Origin of Species by Means of Natural Selection* was published in 1859 and caused a sensation. He spent the remainder of his life pondering and refining his theory. Although he was reluctant to discuss religion, he was an agnostic.

GEORGE ELIOT (Marian Evans) (1819–1880) A leading nineteenth-century novelist, who wrote such masterpieces as *The Mill On the Floss* and *Middlemarch.* She lost her religious faith painfully as a young woman, and remained a determined unbeliever throughout her life.

HERBERT SPENCER (1820–1903) He published *Principles of Psychology* (1855), which contains evolutionary speculation, without the evidence Darwin provided. He put forward ideas of 'social Darwinism' and wrote many works on philosophy, psychology and sociology.

JOSEPH ERNEST RENAN (1823–1892) He was a French Biblical scholar, whose best-known work was the *Life of Jesus*—a naturalistic, historical rather than religious approach. Many works on the history of Christianity included *St. Paul* (1869) and *History of the Israelites* (1887–94).

THOMAS HENRY HUXLEY (1825–1895) A biologist who became professor of natural history at the Royal School of Mines. He became one of the main proponents of Darwin's theory of evolution. At Oxford he debated evolution with Bishop Wilberforce, and declared he would rather be descended from an ape than a bishop. He coined the word 'agnostic'.

SIR LESLIE STEPHEN (1832–1904) He was educated as a Christian and was ordained, but later abandoned the Christian faith. An account of his beliefs was given in *An Agnostic's Apology* (1893). He wrote many essays and historical and literary works. One of his daughters was the distinguished novelist Virginia Woolf.

ANDREW DICKSON WHITE (1832–1918) An American with a very distinguished career as an academic and as a diplomat. He was minister to Berlin and St. Petersburg among other positions. His *History of the Warfare of Science with Theology in Christendom* was an indictment of Christianity which was translated into many languages. He was a theist anxious for the purification of Christianity.

MONCURE CONWAY (1832–1907) An American Methodist and then Unitarian minister, he was an energetic anti-slavery campaigner at the time of the Civil War. He visited Britain to lecture and became a successor of W. J. Fox at the South Place Chapel, which he slowly converted to an ethical society. Among his chief writings were a biography and edition of Thomas Paine and a *Sacred Anthology* looking at religions around the world.

CHARLES BRADLAUGH (1833–1891) A renowned atheist, radical reformer and politician. He edited the *National Reformer* for many years and was the President of the National Secular Society. As a Liberal MP he battled for several years to obtain the right to affirm rather than swear on the Bible on entering Parliament.

ROBERT GREEN INGERSOLL (1833–1899) A lawyer and orator, who conducted an anti-Christian crusade. He disarmed his critics by his persuasive powers. His lectures and pamphlets include *Why Am I an Agnostic?*, *What Is Religion?* and *Some Mistakes of Moses.*

MARK TWAIN (SAMUEL CLEMENS) (1835–1910) The American author of *Tom Sawyer* (1876) and *Huckleberry Finn* (1884)— which gained a world reputation as children's books. He was a prolific journalist and humorist, his writing becoming dark and more sceptical of religion in later years.

SAMUEL BUTLER (1833–1902). Destined for the church, he avoided ordination and became a sheep-farmer in New Zealand. He returned and became a writer. Two satires *Erewhon* and *Erewhon Revisited* were utopian and anti-religious. An autobiographical novel—*The Way of All Flesh* (1903)—was influential.

WILLIAM EDWARD HARTPOLE LECKY (1838–1903) An Irish historian, who became MP for Dublin in 1895. His major historical works include *History of Rationalism* (1865) and *Democracy and Liberty* (1896).

JOHN MORLEY (1838–1923) A man of letters and politician. He was Secretary for Ireland and later Secretary for India, being elevated to the House of Lords. His many literary works include biographies of Voltaire, Diderot, Cobden, and Gladstone.

WILLIAM JAMES (1842–1910) A student of medicine who became a professor of philosophy, then psychology. He placed psychology on a physiological basis and described himself as a 'radical empiricist'. He treated religion and ethics in this way in *Varieties of Religious Experience* (1902).

FRIEDRICH WILHELM NIETZSCHE (1844–1900) The son of a Lutheran pastor, he was a brilliant classicist as a young man. His literary masterpieces include *The Birth of Tragedy* (1872) and *Thus Spoke Zarathustra* (1886), which was profoundly anti-Christian. Poor health and madness accompanied the later part of his life.

WILLIAM KINGDON CLIFFORD (1845–1879) A brilliant mathematician, who became professor of applied mathematics at University College London. He also lectured successfully to popular audiences, but his career was brought to an early close by tuberculosis. His essays include 'The Ethics of Belief' and 'Right and Wrong: the Scientific Ground of their Distinction'.

GEORGE WILLIAM FOOTE (1850–1915) President of the National Secular Society and founder of *The Freethinker* in 1881, of which he remained editor until his death. In 1883 he was prosecuted for blasphemy for publishing a number of comic cartoons satirising Christianity. He was found guilty and given a year's imprisonment—a punishment which was thought scandalously harsh by many.

SIGMUND FREUD (1856–1939) The founder of psychoanalysis, which claimed to uncover repressed fears and sexual desires seething in the unconscious. He caused controversy by a late work on religion—*The Future of an Illusion* (1927).

JOHN DEWEY (1859–1952) An American philosopher and theorist of education, who had a distinguished academic career in American universities. He published many books on psychology, education and philosophy and was known as a pragmatist. In his *Influence of Darwinism on Philosophy* (1910) he said that he was not interested in 'an intelligence that shaped things once for all, but the intelligence which things are even now shaping'.

JOHN BAGNELL BURY (1861–1927) An Irish historian, who became professor of modern history, then Greek, and then modern history again. He wrote many historical works, including *History of Freedom of Thought* (1913), which contained a long section on 'The Growth of Rationalism'.

GOLDSWORTHY LOWES DICKINSON (1862–1932) An influential Cambridge academic, whose books covered ideas of morality and religion, being influenced by Greek life and philosophy. *Religion and Immortality* (1911) delineated his scepticism about an afterlife, and *War: its Nature, Cause and Cure* (1923) indicated his pacifist position.

GEORGE GILBERT AIMÉ MURRAY (1866–1957) He was born in Australia, but educated in England. He became Professor of Greek first in Glasgow, then in Oxford. His translations of Greek tragedy were performed to great acclaim. He was President of the League of Nations Union (1923–1938) and then president of the United Nations Association General Council.

CHAPMAN COHEN (1868–1954) He was President of the National Secular Society from 1915 to 1949 and editor of *The*

Freethinker from 1915 to 1951. In a long life as a freethought leader, he wrote prolifically especially on philosophical subjects and particularly on the theme of materialism.

BERTRAND RUSSELL (1872–1970) A renowned philosopher, mathematician, peace campaigner, and writer. Russell's early philosophical work aimed to underpin the logic of all mathematics. He was imprisoned as a peace campaigner during the First World War and again after demonstrating against the nuclear bomb. His most popular work may be *The History of Western Philosophy* (1945) and he wrote many humanist essays including *Why I Am Not a Christian.*

GEORGE EDWARD MOORE (1873–1958) While a student at Cambridge, he was persuaded by Bertrand Russell to switch from classics to philosophy. His *Principia Ethica* (1903) was the key work in moral philosophy for many years. His concept of goodness included the value of friendship and aesthetic experience—a view which influenced the Bloomsbury group.

ALBERT EINSTEIN (1879–1955) A mathematical physicist, who gained world fame for his special and general theories of relativity (1905 and 1915). As a Bavarian Jew, he left Europe for America following the rise of Hitler. He warned Roosevelt that Germany was developing an atomic bomb and spent much time after the war trying to effect control of the use of atomic weapons.

EDWARD MORGAN FORSTER (1879–1971) A leading twentieth-century novelist, he characterised the morals of English middle-class life in novels such as *Where Angels Fear to Tread* (1905) and *Howards End* (1910). His depiction of colonial India, *Passage to India* (1924), is considered a masterpiece. His novel *Maurice,* written during the First World War and covering the theme of homosexuality, was published posthumously.

HENRY LOUIS MENCKEN (1880–1956) An extremely successful American journalist and prolific writer of books. His series under the head 'The Free Lance' attacked vice crusaders, politicians and 'other such frauds'. He believed deeply in free speech and frequently dealt with the conflict between scientific scepticism and religious belief.

JULIAN HUXLEY (1887–1975) Grandson of T. H. Huxley and a distinguished zoologist who became secretary of the Zoological Society. His writings include *Religion Without Revelation* (1927) and *Towards a New Humanism* (1957). He was the first Director-General of UNESCO (1946–48) and presided over the first conference of the International Humanist and Ethical Union (1952).

M. N. ROY (1887–1954) An Indian activist and philosopher. He fought the British rule, learnt communism in an American library, worked with Lenin in Russia, left Russia just in time, and returned to India where he was arrested by the British authorities. During his years in prison he became a 'radical humanist' and subsequently became leader of the Radical Democratic Party. He believed that humanism must be spread at the grass roots and should completely change society.

BARBARA FRANCES WOOTTON (1897–1988) A social scientist who began her career teaching economics at Girton College Cambridge. She was a research worker for the Labour Party, then followed a distinguished academic career attempting to lay down the scientific principles of social science. She was a magistrate in London and in later years became a well-known broadcaster who made her humanist views quite clear.

GORA (1902–1975) An Indian lecturer in natural science, who gradually challenged religious belief and lost his job for writing an article on atheism. Another job went when he refused to refrain from discussing atheism. He set up the Atheist Centre, where counter-religious propaganda was combined with social work. His children have continued the Atheist Centre, which is flourishing in Vijayada, Andhra Pradesh, today.

SIDNEY HOOK (1902–1989) An American philosopher who spent most of his working life teaching philosophy at New York University. He was outspoken in his atheist naturalism and active in humanist and political issues. His works cover Marxism, of which he was increasingly critical, and secularisation, seen for instance in his *The Quest for Being* (1961), subtitled 'Studies in Naturalism and Humanism'. He was a powerful defender of freedom against every sort of tyranny.

H. J. BLACKHAM (1903–) A leading twentieth-century humanist, who worked first in the ethical movement, then with the British Humanist Association. His interests are philosophical and his books include *Humanism* (1968), *Objections to Humanism* (1963) and *Six Existentialist Thinkers* (1952).

MARGARET KNIGHT (1903–1983) worked in the Psychology Deparwhent of Aberdeen University from 1937 to 1970, alongside her husband, Professor Rex Knight. Together they wrote *A Modern Introduction to Psychology* (1948) and she edited a collection on *William James* (1950). She was an active writer and speaker for the humanist movement, and in 1955 achieved fame when she gave a series of BBC radio talks on non-religious morality and education. These were included in her collection of essays, *Morals Without Religion.* She edited the first edition of the *Humanist Anthology* (1961).

JEAN PAUL SARTRE (1905–1980) A French philosopher, novelist and playwright. He took part in the Resistance during the Second World War and subsequently became well-known as the exponent of atheistic existentialism. He was later active in opposition to the war in Vietnam. His works include *Existentialism and Humanism* (1946), the sequence of novels *Roads to Freedom* (1945-49) and biographies of Genet and Flaubert.

A. J. AYER (1910–1989) The foremost English philosopher to expound the logical positivism coming from the Viennese school of the 1930s. His book *Language, Truth and Logic* (1936) was highly controversial with its criticism of moral and religious ideas. His other books included *The Problem of Knowledge* (1956) and *The Central Questions of Philosophy* (1972).

PETER MEDAWAR (1915–1987) was a biologist who pioneered the development of Immunology. He was professor of zoology at

Birmingham and of comparative anatomy at University College, London, and then director of the National Institute for Medical Research. In 1960 he shared the Nobel Prize for Physiology or Medicine for his work on immunological tolerance, which had great importance in the techniques of grafting tissues and transplanting organs. He wrote several popular books on scientific methods, and was a leading advocate of rational scientific thought.

ALEX COMFORT (1920–) He trained as a doctor, worked as a gerontologist at University College London from 1951 to 1973 and then in California from 1974 to 1980. He has produced a large amount of technical and popular scientific publications and is also a prolific poet and novelist, but he is best known for his writings and broadcasting on sex. He was involved in anarchist and pacifist movements and became one of the prophets of personal and political liberation after the Second World War.

ANTONY FLEW (1923–) He was Professor of Philosophy at Reading University from 1971 to 1982. His essay 'The Presumption of Atheism' is a major contribution to twentieth-century thought on the subject. Many other writings include *A New Approach to Psychical Research* (1953), Hume's Philosophy of Belief (1961) and *God and Philosophy* (1966).

PAUL KURTZ (1925–) A leading American humanist, noted both for his philosophical works and his dynamic leadership of the American and international humanist organisations. His works include *Humanist Manifesto II* (1973), *A Secular Humanist Declaration* (1980), and among his numerous books are *Exuberance: A Philosophy of Happiness* and *The Transcendental Temptation: A Critique of Religion and the Paranormal* (1986).

RICHARD DAWKINS (1941–) A leading scientist in the field of evolution. He has produced two widely influential books, *The Selfish Gene* (1976) and *The Blind Watchmaker* (1988). A pamphlet *Viruses of the Mind* was delivered as the 1992 Voltaire Lecture.

J. BRONOWSKI (1908–1974) He was born in Poland but his family settled in Britain and he was educated at Cambridge. He was a distinguished scientist and also wrote and broadcast on the arts. *The Ascent of Man* was a major 13-part television series first shown in 1973.

DAVID ATTENBOROUGH (1926–) He is a naturalist and broadcaster. His series *Zoo Quest* (1954–64) enabled him to film in many parts of the world. He was Controller of BBC2 from 1965–68 and Director of Programmes (1969–1972). His subsequent series *Life on Earth* (1979), *The Living Planet* (1984) and *The First Eden* (1987) have been widely acclaimed.

Note: the last two entries are out of chronological order, since their extracts provide a fitting conclusion to the anthology.

ACKNOWLEDGEMENTS

Thanks are due to the following for permission to reproduce extracts from copyright works:

George Allen and Unwin Ltd and the Liveright Publishing Corporation for Bertrand Russell, *The Conquest of Happiness;* Allen and Unwin and the Macmillan Co Inc for Arthur Waley's translations of Lao Tzu, Confucius and Mencius; Allen and Unwin and W. W. Norton and Co Inc for Barbara Wootton, *Testament for Social Science;* Allen and Unwin and Simon and Schuster Inc for Bertrand Russell, *Why I Am Not a Christian.*

Appleton-Century Crofts for Andrew White, *A History of the Warfare of Science with Theology in Christendom.*

Edward Arnold Ltd for J. E. McTaggart, *Some Dogmas of Religion.* Edward Arnold Ltd for E. M. Forster's extracts from *Two Careers for Democracy.*

BBC Enterprises Ltd for extract from J. Bronowski's *The Ascent of Man.*

The Beacon Press, Boston, and Jonathan Cape Ltd for Einstein, 'The Laws of Science and the Laws of Ethics'(preface to Philipp Frank, *Relativity. A Richer Truth*).

The Bodley Head Ltd for Einstein, *The World as I See It,* translated by Alan Harris.

The Cambridge University Press for Origen, *Contra Celsum,* translated by H. Chadwick, and G. E. Moore, *Principia Ethica.*

The Clarendon Press, Oxford, for Cyril Bailey's translation of Epicurus and A. S. L. Farquharson's translation of Marcus Aurelius.

Madame Daryush for translations of Marcus Aurelius and Spinoza by Robert Bridges.

Dobson Books Ltd for Margaret Knight, *Morals without Religion.*

Harper Collins Ltd and Mr David Attenborough for extract from *Life on Earth.*

William Heinemann Ltd for translations of Cicero by H. Rackham, and of Seneca by J. W. Basore and R. M. Gummere, in the Loeb Classical Library; Heinemann, Doubleday and Co Inc.

The Hogarth Press Ltd for Freud, *The Future of an Illusion.* Macmillan and Co Ltd for John Morley, *On Compromise.*

Lady Medawar for the extract from Peter Medawar's *The Limits of Silence.*

Methuen and Co Ltd and the University of Michigan Press for G. Lowes Dickinson, *The Greek View of Life.*

Methuen and Co for the extract from J. P. Sartre's *Existentialism and Humanism.*

The New American Library of World Literature Inc for Moses Hadas's translation of Plutarch (Mentor Books: *On Love, The Family, and the Good Life: Selected Essays by Plutarch*).

Penguin Books Ltd for R. E. Latham's translation of Lucretius, *On the Nature of the Universe.*

Penguin Books and Mr H. J. Blackham for an extract from *Humanism.*

Prometheus Books, USA, for 'Humanism and Moral Education' by Paul Kurtz and 'The Snare of Definitions' by Sydney Hook, both from *The Humanist Alternative.*

The Rationalist Press Association for an extract from Antony Flew's *The Presumption of Atheism.*

Routledge and Kegan Paul Ltd for H. L. Mencken, *Treatise on Right and Wrong.*

Williams and Norgate Ltd (Ernest Benn Ltd) for J. B. Bury, *A History of Freedom of Thought.*

The Yale University Press for John Dewey, *A Common Faith.*